Experts and the Will of the People

"Collins, Evans, Durant, and Weinel set out convincingly, in crystal clear language, why democracies need experts and expert knowledge. They make a rock solid case for the necessity of communities of experts in democratic societies and for the value of esoteric knowledge developed and nurtured within these communities. In doing so, they strike a blow against the current rise of populism in the political arena and against theories in Science & Technology Studies that treat expert knowledge as undermining of democratic agency. This book brings the 'Third Wave' studies of expertise and experience to bear in an impressive way on central problems of political theory that are also matters of urgent public concern as democracies turn toward populism and authoritarianism."
—Charles Thorpe, Professor, *Sociology and Science Studies, University of California, San Diego*

Harry Collins • Robert Evans
Darrin Durant • Martin Weinel

Experts and the Will of the People

Society, Populism and Science

Harry Collins
School of Social Sciences
Cardiff University
Cardiff, UK

Robert Evans
School of Social Sciences
Cardiff University
Cardiff, UK

Darrin Durant
Historical & Philosophical Studies
University of Melbourne
Melbourne, VIC, Australia

Martin Weinel
School of Social Sciences
Cardiff University
Cardiff, UK

ISBN 978-3-030-26982-1   ISBN 978-3-030-26983-8   (eBook)
https://doi.org/10.1007/978-3-030-26983-8

This Palgrave Pivot imprint is published by the registered company Springer Nature Switzerland AG.
The registered company address is: Gewerbestrasse 11, 6330 Cham, Switzerland

BOOK ABSTRACTS

CHAPTER 1: INTRODUCTION: PLURALIST DEMOCRACY, POPULISM AND EXPERTISE

The rise of populism in the West has led to attacks on scientific expertise. We explain populism through its contrast with pluralist democracy and explain why populists attack scientific expertise. Populism treats the losers at the ballot box and anyone who stands in the way of the government, including scientific experts, as traitors. In contrast, pluralist democracy accommodates minority views by limiting the power of government with 'checks and balances'. Contemporary science and technology studies (STS) erodes the cultural importance of scientific expertise and, unwittingly supports the rise of populism. STS must re-think the justification of scientific expertise and its role in society without sacrificing its deep insights into the social nature of science; it should no longer simply celebrate the erosion of sciences cultural pre-eminence.

CHAPTER 2: WHAT IS SOCIETY?

Societies are distinguished by what their citizens take for granted. In 'Western societies' most citizens agree, among other things, about the need for regular elections with near-universal franchises, how to treat strangers, the poor and the sick. These understandings are sedimented in the course of socialisation and constitute the *organic face* of societies; there is so much agreement that such things don't usually feature in political manifestos. Citizens record more detailed, varying, and self-conscious choices in elections, giving rise to the *enumerative face* of societies. Populism deliberately confuses the enumerative face with the organic face. Citizens can make non-democratic leaders accountable only if they know what democracy means; this is the law of conservation of democracy.

CHAPTER 3: WHAT IS DEMOCRACY?

There are many forms of democracy. Importantly, is there continual accounting to the public via referendums—'direct democracy'—or do the people choose representatives who govern relatively independently between elections? It is natural in representative democracy for experts to be consulted by the elected government, whereas if directness is the ideal, experts can look like unaccountable elites. Under 'pluralist democracy' governments' power is limited by institutional 'checks and balances', such as the judiciary, the free press and alternative parliamentary chambers, ensuring that minorities and minority opinions are not completely suppressed. Checks and balances require experts. There are many other dimensions of democracies including voting systems and the degree of devolution, but an uncritical advocacy of 'rule by the people' is antagonistic to pluralist democracy.

CHAPTER 4: WHAT IS POPULISM?

Populism contrasts clearly with pluralist democracy. By treating the result of elections as representing 'the will of the people', populism misrepresents the enumerative face of society as the organic face and defines all opposition to the elected government as traitorous. Minorities, and the institutions and experts upon which the checks and balance of pluralist democracy depend, are, therefore, attacked by populist leaders. Populist leaders claim that their actions, however dictatorial, and however much they favour a specific group in society, are democratic—they represent the will of the people. Because populism, in its championing of the people, is anti-elitist, some commentators consider it can enliven democracy. In today's world, however, the dangers are obvious: attacks on minorities and the control of what counts as expertise.

CHAPTER 5: WHAT IS SCIENCE?

Since the early 1970s, in social studies of science and technology (STS), the 'logic of scientific discovery' has been displaced by detailed examinations of science in practice; this has eroded the cultural position of scientific expertise. Furthermore, the 'crown jewels' of science, Newtonian physics and the like, are no longer accepted as justifying science's contribution to citizens' more diffuse technical concerns. Scientific expertise now seems more fallible, less removed from ordinary decision-making and less insulated from political and social forces. Populist leaders, who attack scientific expertise because it limits their power, can draw on these ideas. STS must stop celebrating the erosion of scientific expertise and, without sacrificing the new insights, rethink the justification for the role of science in democratic societies.

CHAPTER 6: HOW DOES SCIENCE FIT INTO SOCIETY? THE FRACTAL MODEL

According to Studies of Expertise and Experience (SEE), expertise is socialisation into an expert domain. Society consists of many expert domains of different extent, some small and esoteric, some, like language, large and ubiquitous. Expert domains overlap and are embedded within each other like a fractal. Citizens possess 'ubiquitous meta-expertise' which enables them choose domains when seeking expert opinions—such as whether a vaccine is safe. In such cases, citizens must be ready to treat domains of scientific expertise as more valuable than power or celebrity if we are to avoid dystopia and maintain pluralistic democracy with its checks and balances. Democracies depend on their citizens—'the law of conservation of democracy'; this means we need more civic education to safeguard the future.

CONTENTS

LIST OF FIGURES

CHAPTER 1

Introduction: Pluralist Democracy, Populism and Expertise

Abstract The rise of populism in the West has led to attacks on scientific expertise. We explain populism through its contrast with pluralist democracy and explain why populists attack scientific expertise. Populism treats the losers at the ballot box and anyone who stands in the way of the government, including scientific experts, as traitors. In contrast, pluralist democracy accommodates minority views by limiting the power of government with 'checks and balances'. Contemporary science and technology studies (STS) erodes the cultural importance of scientific expertise and unwittingly supports the rise of populism. STS must re-think the justification of scientific expertise and its role in society without sacrificing its deep insights into the social nature of science; it should no longer simply celebrate the erosion of sciences cultural pre-eminence.

Keywords Populism • Pluralist democracy • Scientific expertise • Checks and balances • Science and technology studies (STS)

In 1911, to explore the structure of the atom, Rutherford bombarded gold foil with the sub-atomic missiles produced by radioactivity and watched what happened. That's a good way to investigate the world—an impact can reveal the structure of what is being hit. In social science the idea is known as a 'breaching experiment': disturb the smooth running of ordinary life with outrageous behaviour and life's hidden order shows

© The Author(s) 2020   1
H. Collins et al., *Experts and the Will of the People*,
https://doi.org/10.1007/978-3-030-26983-8_1

itself.[1] We can think of US President, Donald Trump, as engaged in a series of inadvertent breaching experiments and these, along with similar recent shocks in other Western democracies, create an opportunity for a deeper understanding of the political world we inhabit. For example, it has been clearly revealed that the formal constitution of the United States rests on an unwritten constitution. Thanks to Trump's political missiles, we can see that, up to now, the unwritten constitution includes the expectation that presidents will disclose their tax returns, will divest themselves of private business interests, will not appoint unqualified members of their family as senior advisors, will not sack the Director of the FBI at will, will not attack institutions by such actions as appointing opponents of environmental protection to the Environmental Protection Agency, and will refrain from endorsing those accused of child molesting for the US Senate.[2] This election and its aftermath are showing us, anew, how democracy works, or used to work.

A New Definition of Populism

Trump's predations on democratic traditions are often seen as a symptom of 'populism' but, like 'democracy' and many other political terms, populism means different things to different people. Here we are going to put forward a new and simple definition of populism which explains most of what is going on right now in Western democracies. The new definition contrasts populism with a version of democracy which we and others call 'pluralist'. We define populism by its contrast with pluralist democracy and we define pluralist democracy by its contrast with populism. Do you want to understand the rhetoric of Britain's Brexiteers? Do you want to understand what is meant by 'the will of the people'? These definitions do the job. And, crucially, they feed into our explanation of the role of scientific

---

[1] The classic source for this idea is the work of sociologist Harold Garfinkel (Garfinkel 2011). For instance, he asked students to behave as if they were guests in a hotel when they were at home so as to uncover the normal rules of family life.

[2] Though he does not use the term 'breaching experiment' this argument is the burden of an article by Jonathan Freedland (2017) writing in the *Guardian*. Students of philosophy, sociology and social studies of science should already know that the written constitution is supported by an unwritten constitution since, as the philosopher Wittgenstein (1953) explains, 'rules do not contain the rules for their own application', something that is also evident in sociological studies of bureaucracy (Gouldner 1954). For unwritten norms of American democratic institutions, see Levitsky and Ziblatt (2018, chap. 6).

expertise in democracies: scientific expertise is one of the checks and balances in pluralist democracies and that is why populists attack scientific expertise just as they attack the other checks and balances.

The contrast between pluralist democracy and populism arises out of an understanding of the nature of society. Societies are constituted by collective agreements about how they run and what they value. For example, many Western societies are defined by their agreement to re-elect their governments in a fair way every few years with a near universal franchise. There is common agreement about what counts as 'fair' and common agreement about what counts as lawful behaviour, and what counts as appropriate treatment of family and strangers; it is commonly agreed that the work of the police should be open and accountable and that citizens should not be refused medical treatment on the grounds of ethnicity or poverty. Not every person in the society has to agree to these things but the huge majority accepts them, often without thinking about it, and in the same way they agree, without thinking, to a much longer list of such things. This set of, mostly, *tacit* agreements, is what gives a society its particular character. This is what we call the 'organic' face of a society; the organic face is what makes a society the kind of animal it is and makes it that there are huge differences among the multitude of societies that populate the world even though they are all peopled by biologically similar human beings. The organic face of a society is relatively stable, normally changing only slowly, though the fact that it can change means there will always be some overlap at the boundary of the organic face and more ordinary preferences. Of course, at times of social revolution there is a sudden and sometimes violent change in the organic face.

In contrast, within the generally agreed framework that defines a 'Western' democracy, regular elections offer citizens choices on more detailed policy issues that decide how the ways of being that make up the organic face should be put into practice. These policy issues divide rather than unite the society and sometimes they are organised by political parties into broader patterns of difference. Because the aggregate of citizens' choices is indicated by counting votes at elections we call the outcome of such exercises the 'enumerative face' of a society. Because the enumerative face can reveal a close balance of divided opinion it is quite normal for governing power chosen through the enumerative process to change hands at elections.

Pluralist democracies are defined by their respect for the preferences that lose out in the enumerative process. Though a government will be elected, the governing power will moderate its policies to take account of the fact that there is a substantial body of citizens whose choices were not successful at the ballot box. To stop governments losing sight, under the pressure of events, of their responsibility to those who did not win the vote, pluralist democracies have institutions that act as 'checks and balances' on the government such as a legally protected parliamentary opposition parties, competing parliamentary chambers—upper houses or the competition between Congress and Senate—an independent legal system and a free press. Our new and simple definition of populism is that *a populist portrays the outcome of an enumerative process as giving rise to a new organic face of society.*

The populist move is often graphically expressed by claiming that the result of an election represents 'the will of the people': the will of the people is presented as something organic not enumerative. Once the idea of an organic will of the people gains currency it licences the treatment of minority views as traitorous and it legitimates the suppression of the institutions that provide checks and balances. With this contrast in mind we can immediately understand the way events have been unfolding recently in the Western World. For instance, in the UK we can understand the way the 17.4 million people who voted 'leave' in the 2016 Brexit referendum have been continually spoken of by ruthless 'Brexiteers' as expressing 'the will of the people' even though 16.1 million voted the opposite way and the total voting for leave was only about 37% of those who were registered to vote with 35% voting the other way; we can understand why on the 4th November 2016, after three judges had ruled that the consent of parliament was needed to begin the Brexit process, the right-wing nationalist newspaper *The Daily Mail,* pictured the judges on their front page with the headline 'Enemies of the People'; and we can understand why on the 21st March 2019, a desperate Prime-Minster, Theresa May addressed the nation claiming that she understood what the people wanted and parliament was standing in her way and preventing her from executing the nation's will.

Finally, what this new definition puts us in a position to claim is that the institutions that provide scientific and technological expertise are, like the judiciary and the free press, central to pluralist democracies since they provide a check and balance which limits the power of elected leaders to proclaim that their interpretations of the natural and social landscape are mandated by the people. That this is how these institutions work has been most obviously demonstrated by more of the American leadership's breaching experiments: Donald Trump's claims in respect of climate change and his entourage's attempts to counter scientific expertise with alternative facts in a post-truth world. We see him not just appointing an environmental critic to be the head of an environmental protection agency, but denying the validity of climate science itself while his advisor shamelessly assumed mathematical authority over the numbers attending the President's inauguration.

Once the role of scientific expertise is understood in terms of the tension between pluralist democracy and populism, we can ask new kinds of questions about the contribution of social studies of science to the contemporary political environment. The position we take is that there is a choice to be made. The naturalistic understanding of the methods of science that has grown since the early 1970s has led to some erosion of science's cultural authority that cannot be reversed. The political consequences of this are not, however, as clear as many take them to be. The choice to be made is between celebrating and *embracing* the erosion of science's cultural and political status or *rethinking* the way that status is to be justified under the new understanding of what science is. In sum, the choice is between what we will call the '*embrace* persuasion' and the '*rethink* persuasion'. We argue that the contemporary political climate brings fresh urgency to the need to rethink science's status in democracies.

THE STRUCTURE OF THE BOOK

The rest of the book consists of a more detailed exposition of these ideas. We fill out our analysis of the nature of societies in Chap. 2. We talk about the different existing definitions of democracy (Chap. 3) and the different existing definitions of populism (Chap. 4). One can see why democracy and populism need to be untangled since both can be said to be 'rule by the people' and some analysts consider that a dose of populism is good for democracy. And we need to explain how it is that the value of scientific expertise, the superiority of which was once taken to be so obvious that such a view was part of the organic face of Western societies, has come to be questioned so that it is no longer an automatic check and balance on the power of governments (Chap. 5).[3] Indeed, some analysts believe that

[3] We are in a good position to explain this as the authors of this book were contributors to the transformation of the understanding of science, at least as it played out among academics.

scientific expertise is in tension with democracy since scientific judgements are made by elites and are impenetrable by the electorate whose democratic rights they necessarily violate. We will explain that there is no more tension here than there is with legal expertise or with the expertise of civil servants. We expect legal professionals and civil servants to have capabilities in their fields beyond those of the ordinary citizen but this is taken to strengthen democracy rather than push the ordinary citizen out into the non-democratic cold. That said, *technocracy* is a danger; technocracy is when scientific experts start to make political decisions rather than making a contribution to political decisions. But, once the danger is understood, putting a high valuation on scientific expertise does not lead to technocracy.

To anticipate some of the more detailed discussion of democracy, there are theoretical versions of democracy that are not pluralist yet still utopian such as an ideal communism which, because of its stress on equality, appeals to many. In practice, however, they do not seem to have turned out well so we are ignoring them for practical purposes. Furthermore, while endorsing pluralist democracy, we do not mean to imply acceptance of the corruption, dishonesty, gerrymandering and worse, that are present in many existing democracies. The point is that pluralism is something we want from democracies irrespective of how well they are working in other respects. The idea and the term are important because ways of governing which may be corrupt in many ways, including having no respect for minority views, are often described by powerful leaders as 'democratic' because they, in some sense, reflect the will of the people. We recognise that some populist movements grow out of disillusion with the working of democracy as it is encountered but this does not mean we should forget about how we would like society to be governed.

Our definition of pluralist democracy is close to 'liberal democracy' but avoiding that term saves us from disputes such as that concerning the relative status of economic rights and civil rights: what is the relative weighting of protection for independent activity in markets, the right to own property and State support for the enforcing of contracts versus equality of opportunity, religious freedom, and social justice.

Acting within pluralist democracies, then, governments try to accommodate minority rights and views. What is meant by 'accommodate' is a complicated issue in its own right. For example, suppose the majority in a country vote for representatives who will strongly encourage a regime of universal vaccination so as to establish herd immunity against certain diseases. At the same time, a sizeable minority vote the other way. The minority cannot simply be given the right not to vaccinate because that would sabotage the desired herd immunity and the outcome would be rule by the minority! But a moderate democracy will still listen to the minority group, remaining attentive to their value-preferences and the explanations they offer for their opposition, and keep in mind the *possibility* of reversing the policy at some time should understanding of the powers and dangers of vaccines change in the direction of the minority; to that extent, at least, they would *accommodate* the opposition to the policy. We'll just stick with saying that 'accommodate' means trying to find ways to take minority opinions into account with all the unresolved paradoxes, such as tolerance of intolerance, that this might imply.

We also introduce what we call 'The Law of Conservation of Democracy', which says that citizens have to understand the nature of democracy if the democracies they live in are to last: if citizens don't know what democracy means then they cannot recognise violations and call them to account.

Again, anticipating the main text, it cannot be the case that more citizen consultation is always equivalent to more democracy because moving too far in that direction would destroy the institutional checks and balances that depend on *experts*. Once more, vaccination is a touchstone. And that, we will argue, is an example of where scientific experts come in. The start of any solution to the enigmatic relationship of expertise and democracy is the realization that while, ideally, citizens, usually through their representatives, will have the *last word* when it comes to deciding matters involving policy questions that turn on esoteric knowledge, in a pluralist democracy citizens and experts will be part of a distribution of power which also recognises where esoteric knowledge is to be found. This might seem obvious but the contribution expertise makes to pluralist democracy is badly misunderstood, especially by those who treat it as a threat to democratic rights.

In Chap. 5 we will explain in more detail what science is—something we have only begun to understand in anything other than 'cartoon' form, since the 1970s. The transformation of our understanding of science that came with studies of the day-to-day work of scientists we will refer to as the 'watershed' in understanding science. The new analysis of science has to be fed into the understanding of science's various roles in society, not least its relationship to democracy. A widespread and salient consequence of the post-watershed analysis of science is the vocal endorsement of the inevitable intermingling of social and political forces with science; science can no longer be seen as an institution that provides answers that are purely objective, implying absolute independence from political and social pressures on the ordinary lives of the scientists that provide them. But if this kind of view 'escapes into the wild' without modification it could extinguish science's role as a limit on the erosion of democracy because science will come to be seen simply as a continuation of politics rather than a potential challenge to political power. Today, when the political environment is no longer as benign as it has been for the last 50 years, the dangers are evident; powerful, enriching and enlightening as the post-watershed analyses have been, we now need to build on them in ways that respond to recent events and re-establish science's right to challenge power; we need this now in the way the democracies needed it in the 1930s.

As explained, the contemporary rise of populism, or populist tendencies, in some Western democracies, especially the USA, with associated attacks on expertise, is what triggered the writing of this book. Chapter 6 is the key concluding chapter and adds more detail to what has been anticipated in this Introduction: it sets out how scientific expertise fits into pluralist democracies and looks at what needs to change if such democracies are to be robust. We introduce the 'fractal model of society' as the context for the argument. If the Law of Conservation of Democracy is right, then civic education is the key to a lasting democracy. Civic education will include the idea of pluralist democracy as opposed to the simple power of the ballot box and will explain the nature of citizens' various sources of information and understanding, including the balance of expert opinion versus the internet and social media. In today's society this kind of understanding is under strain as expert elites are presented as untrustworthy and conspiracy theories flourish, but we have to keep the longer term future in mind; if we don't find a way of imparting this deeper kind of understanding to the citizenry the future is bleak. Part of civic education will be about the way groups of scientific and other experts fit into society; the fractal model provides an outline framework for talking about it. In an earlier book Collins and Evans introduce a more specific idea: a new institution, called 'The Owls'. This would reconcile social science and natural science in providing an account of the strength and substance of scientific consensus in disputed domains; the account is then passed to the political sphere as a non-determining element in policy formation. But institutions cannot work on their own; citizen-understanding has to form the substance of democracy. This book is our attempt to have an influence on what, we hope, will one day be what everyone understands.

REFERENCES

Freedland, Jonathan. 2017. The Year of Trump Has Laid Bare the US Constitution's Serious Flaws. *The Guardian*, December 30, UK edition, sec. Opinion.

Garfinkel, Harold. 2011. *Studies in Ethnomethodology*. Reprinted. Cambridge: Polity Press.

Gouldner, Alvin, W. 1954. *Patterns of Industrial Bureaucracy*. New York: Free Press.

Levitsky, Steven, and Daniel Ziblatt. 2018. *How Democracies Die*. 1st ed. New York: Crown.

Wittgenstein, Ludwig. 1953. *Philosophical Investigations*. Translated by G.E.M Anscombe. Oxford: Blackwell.

CHAPTER 2

What Is Society?

Abstract Societies are distinguished by what their citizens take for granted. In 'Western societies' most citizens agree, among other things, about the need for regular elections with near-universal franchises, how to treat strangers, the poor and the sick. These understandings are sedimented in the course of socialisation and constitute the *organic face* of societies; there is so much agreement that such things don't usually feature in political manifestos. Citizens record more detailed, varying, and self-conscious choices in elections, giving rise to the *enumerative face* of societies. Populism deliberately confuses the enumerative face with the organic face. Citizens can make non-democratic leaders accountable only if they know what democracy means; this is the law of conservation of democracy.

Keywords Nature of society • Organic face • Enumerative face • Populism • Conservation of democracy

To understand how populism works we need to understand how society works: every social group has an organic face in which the society and the people in it can be treated as one collective, and an individual face where persons make relatively free choices from among those that the social group makes available. Populism arises when individual choices are 'enumerated' and then the majority choice is treated as representing the

© The Author(s) 2020   11
H. Collins et al., *Experts and the Will of the People*,
https://doi.org/10.1007/978-3-030-26983-8_2

organic face of society. For most of the Twentieth Century two concepts of the good society—capitalism and communism—were at war with each other. That each side should be convinced that it was right is unsurprising since they each reflect one of two irreducible aspects of every society, individual choice and collective uniformity; human societies are both individualistic and collective, with the latter creating the conditions for the former. Ideologues on both sides see only one aspect as the key to a good society, refusing to see the way each aspect depends upon the other. The champions of free market capitalism insist that individual choice and the opportunity to express it are basic human rights and only by guaranteeing these will efficient markets give rise to the greatest benefit for the greatest number; even though the cost might be growing inequality in society, the lowest stratum will still be better off than they would under a more constrained system. The champions of state control insist that only by remoulding human character into a less competitive and more cooperative form will it become possible for humans to work together efficiently for the good of everyone, eliminating the evil pathology of the division between rich and poor. As we now know, neither side is completely right but both sides are partly right. On the one hand, we know that state control without markets is inefficient and seems to give rise to ruthlessness and corruption at the centre; on the other hand, we know that uncontrolled markets themselves give rise to corruption that destroys their efficiency and to levels of inequality that destroy societies. And we ought to understand that the notion of complete freedom for individuals is nonsensical because individuals can be free, in so far as they are free, only within the cultural constraints of a society. A condition of freedom of speech is being able to speak and be understood. But the ability to speak comes from the collective contributions of all the members of the society whose language you use. When we were young we were constrained to speak the language of our upbringing, or maybe, in special circumstances, there were two, or even more, languages of upbringing, but none of us have ever been simply free to speak in any language we choose to speak at whim. The constraints and enablings of language can stand for all the cultural abilities we draw on from the 'collectivities' in which we are embedded and that enable us to live at all. We'll explore these points in more detail as this chapter unfolds.

The same conflict is reflected in, and generated by, academic discourse. On the one hand, it is said that individual freedom is the essence of human life as shown by our emergence from the slime as a result of unconstrained competition under evolutionary forces that are responsible for the development of morality and enlightenment in general. Humans when left to compete among themselves will produce a freedom-based civilization through interaction with the World; the science of evolution can explain it all. On the other side, civilization is seen to start with the moral insights of the great religions and, whether we are religious observers or not, the culture to which they are an input is key to what we and our societies are. Under this model, evolutionary processes can give rise only to animal societies while human societies develop when culture shapes us through common understanding—a life that is markedly different from society to society as the wide range of different possible cultures demonstrates. Once more, neither side is completely right. Society and societies can be explained only if we take into account both their bottom up, universal elements, and their top down inputs—the individual and the collective. The individual is itself a social product.

This is the context that helps us see that, when they vote, the ordinary people in a modern democratic society might be thinking as individuals but the very possibility that they can think meaningfully arises out of circumstances that are put in place and maintained collectively. Every act of a citizen has these two faces and pathologies occur when one face is confused with the other.

Two Faces of Language

As we will see in Chap. 5, in the Twentieth Century it came to be understood that the findings of science were subject to 'interpretative flexibility', but this was just part of a broad intellectual movement concerned with the varied interpretation of everything as opposed to its fixedness. The heart of this movement, though the inspiration for only some of it, was probably French literary criticism and the iconic statement was made by Roland Barthes—'the author is dead'. What he meant was that once the words were on paper the interpretation was in the hands of the reader and the reader's interpretation would be set in the current social context. The meaning of words changed continually as social context changed and readers changed; the author could do nothing but spin in the grave—his or her intentions were not what gave a text meaning, it was readers' interpretations. And, as authors often discover, you don't even have to be dead to be buried and bizarrely or maliciously reinterpreted.

A great deal of productive academic work arose from the insight about the possibility of endless interpretation and reinterpretation. Academics found they could 'deconstruct' almost anything and many approaches to this task became subsumed under the label 'post-modernism'. The whole of language, not just text, was seen as being a matter of the consumers' 'construction' of meaning with nothing fixed.

But there must be more to it than this. There are two other aspects to the interpretation of text. Consider the following sentence:

The trophy does not fit the brown suitcase because it is too small.[1]

The question is, what is too small, the suitcase or the trophy? Nearly every English speaker, or inhabitant of Western society for that matter, will think the sentence implies that the suitcase is too small. That is the first aspect of the inflexibility of interpretation—nearly everyone reads things the same way and the fact that readers share an interpretation of nearly everything allows trouble-free communication most of the time. This is the case because of the sharing of a culture—we understand trophies and suitcases in a top-down way, and likewise we understand what one can do with them and what we mean by 'fit'. Communication depends on similarities of cultural context and, therefore, a top down propensity to interpret in the same way in spite of the potential for interpretative flexibility that is pretty well everywhere. So, the author cannot be quite as dead as Barthes said.

Where is the potential for interpretative flexibility in this case? Well, someone could take it that the trophy was too small and therefore if placed in the suitcase would rattle about, this still being compatible with the idea of it 'not fitting'. That is the second aspect of the case—it does allow for a minority to choose to interpret in a way different to the majority but without being wrong, and the author can do nothing about it.

The second aspect of inflexibility, which is not very important for what we are working out here but is worth pointing out in passing because so many academics are confused about it, is that the sentence, about the trophy and the suitcase, interpretatively flexible though it is, doesn't allow us to interpret it very easily as meaning 'the cat ate my aunt's pen' or an

---

[1] This sentence, when presented with the option of changing 'big' to 'small', so as to change the tacitly understood reference of the pronoun, is known as a Winograd schema. These are first explained as a problem for artificial intelligence in Terry Winograd's PhD thesis: 'Procedures as a representation for data in a computer program for understanding natural language', Massachusetts Institute of Technology, 1971 (p. 11).

indefinite number of other possibilities. In other words, the words them-selves have a certain 'affordance' or range of affordances which seem to be found in the text itself. Furthermore, in so far as determined individuals can interpret the sentence in more than one way (if not any way they like), this very differential interpretability depends on different individual's common reading of the symbols that make it up: everyone who can read the language sees the 't's as 't's, the 'h's as 'h's, the 'e's as 'e's, and the 'a's as 'a's. Were that not the case, there would be no talk of differential inter-pretability because there would be nothing fixed to interpret differently. So, in several ways, the variable and relativistic is parasitical on the fixed and universal, or near fixed and near universal.[2]

There is something to be learned from this analysis about the way the public makes political choices. This is that, just as nearly everybody in Western societies will interpret that sentence about the trophy and the suitcase in the same way, pretty well all the members of a society will share a huge body of tacit knowledge and understandings including political knowledge and understanding. It is this shared set of understanding and tacit agreements about how life ought to be lived that constitutes a society and it is differences in what is shared that separate one society from another. This is the subject of the 'sociology of knowledge'.[3]

This idea has been written about in many places by one or two of the current authors, but it is such a vital idea that we need to sketch it out again here while apologising to those for whom both the idea and the examples will be familiar.[4] At least let us begin in a newish way—with lan-guage. We have already seen that common culture leads nearly all of us to see the pronoun 'it' in the sentence about trophies and suitcases as refer-ring to the suitcase. Some aspects of language exhibit this feature still more strongly: we'll call it 'uniformity'.[5] Thus pretty well every native English speaker tends to put the verb in the middle of the sentence rather than the end: we do not say 'pretty well every native English speaker tends, the verb, at the end of the sentence to put'. To know where native English speakers put the verb, there is no need to carry out a survey, just listening to one or two haphazardly chosen English speakers is enough. This is

---

[2] See Collins (2018).

[3] Alternatively, it can be thought of in terms of Durkheim's sociology or Wittgenstein's notion of form of life. Durkheim (1915, 2013), Wittgenstein (1953), Winch (1964).

[4] Collins (1992) and Collins and Evans (2017a).

[5] For the idea of uniformity, see Collins and Evans (2017b).

because English, and that includes its typical verb placement, is the property of English-speaking society as a whole and not the property of any
individual. Individuals cannot choose to put the verb at the end of the
sentence—well they could with enough effort but people would think
they were crazy and they would have difficulty circulating in English-
speaking society. Furthermore, when they were children and were learning
English, these English speakers did not *choose* to put the verb in the middle
of the sentence and were almost certainly unaware that they were putting
the verb in the middle of the sentence—that piece of tacit knowledge
came with becoming an English speaker. Indeed, children growing up in
English speaking society do not choose to speak English and, at a pre-
school age, most of them probably do not know they are speaking
English—it just comes with living in English-speaking society. An awful
lot of our culture and our understanding of what is in the world and how
to behave in the world comes to us in the same way; unconsciously,
through socialisation. We absorb these ways of being while remaining as
unaware of them as a fish is unaware that it swims in water: our culture is
our medium and should we have been brought up somewhere else, the
things we would know and do without thinking about them would probably be quite different.

Though there are many routes into this way of thinking, the source that
happens to be our starting point is Wittgenstein's idea of 'form of life'.
The Wittgensteinian philosopher, Peter Winch, expressed the idea in
terms of the development of the germ theory of disease, which represented the establishment of a new element of culture.[6] Now that the germ
theory is established we see surgeons engaging in ritualistic-looking scrubbing and cleansing before they operate. All that scrubbing is part and
parcel of our notion of germ—it shows what germs are: entities too small
to see. We never see the germs, only the scrubbing and we believe in them
only because they are part of cultural sea in which we swim, while at the
same time the scrubbing makes no sense without the notion of germ. So
the idea of germs and the practice of scrubbing come together. We
couldn't have hygiene without the idea of germs, but we couldn't have the

---

[6]Wittgenstein (1953) and Winch (1958). In terms of sociological theory, these kinds of
organic or uniform choices correspond to the approach of Emile Durkheim, one of the
'founding fathers' of sociology, who argued that sociology should be concerned with those
aspects of societies that transcend individuals and provide the structure within which they live
out their lives.

idea of germs without the scrubbing—this is the way our life comes to have meaning. This is why Wittgenstein could say that we should ask for the use of a word, not for its meaning—the meaning of a word was in its use. We might say that dictionaries, in trying to list meanings are sketching uses and creating a shallow description of cultures. Cultures, to repeat, differ: in some there are witches, in some there are mortgages, in some the stars control the fates of princes, in others black holes are observed by the emission of gravitational waves. Crucially, within cultures there are smaller cultures and within these yet further sub-cultures and so on, with each difference between cultures or sub-cultures a potential source of disagreement. This is what we will call the 'fractal model' of societies and we will return to it in Chap. 6.

In seeing how we learn language we are seeing how we learn cultures in general. As already noted, most of what we acquire as culture we acquire without even knowing we are acquiring it. Only later in life, if we receive an education that encourages us to reflect, or if we are sufficiently exposed to other cultures through travel or books or mass media, are we able to gain some inkling of the extent to which our very selves have been constructed out of influences of which we are unaware. Those lucky enough, or unlucky enough, to have encountered the sociology of knowledge will be aware of the disorientating effect of the discovery that most of the things one thinks one believes because they are true, one actually believes because that is how one has been socialized in the place one has been born and grown up. This does not mean that any way of growing up is as good as any other—once we grow up and become aware that life works this way, we still have to make choices about what we count as a good way to live and what as a bad way to live. In this book, even though we realise that this choice has been made possible, and even easy, by the way we, the authors, have been brought up, we are self-consciously choosing pluralist democracy as a good way to live. And, following up from an earlier analysis, we are self-consciously choosing honesty, conscientiousness, a willingness to listen to criticism and 'universalism'—a refusal to count race, ethnicity or gender rather than competence where claims about the nature of the world are concerned—as essential inputs to democracy and to science.[7]

---

[7] The previous analysis is Collins and Evans (2017a); that work presents a much-expanded list of the norms of values of science from which we have selected just four for this abbreviated treatment. Some of the political overtones of this approach to universalism, for instance its implications for 'identity politics' and the giving of reasons in public debate, were foregrounded in Durant (2011).

CONSTITUTIVE AND ENUMERATIVE POPULAR CHOICE

We should now be able to see still more clearly why, as explained in the Introduction, citizens make two kinds of choices as they contribute to the shape of a society. One of these kinds of 'choice' is collective in an organic kind of way[8]; we can expect it to be 'uniform' across the society and it is mostly not really a matter of self-conscious choosing but of citizens' 'taken-for-granted-reality'—the kind of way of being in the world that constitutes the society, or form of life, which the citizen inhabits.[9] If caused to reflect upon their lives, and describe the way they live, and prefer to live, nearly all citizens would answer in the same or a similar way in these respects. This kind of choice runs from where you put the verb in the sentence, to whether you think it is important to identify witches using oracular means, to how near you walk to others on an empty pavement (sidewalk), and whether you believe the Prime Minister or President of a country is entitled to use their office to favour the business interests of themselves and their families. These are examples of what can be found in the organic face of society—something that is more than adding up individual choices but, on the contrary, something metaphysically collective that, to repeat, gives rise to what would be the almost exclusive choice of individual members of a society, were they ever asked to reflect and choose. We will use the adjectives, 'organic', 'metaphysical', 'constitutive', and 'formative' interchangeably when talking about the collective ways we act, including the very act of voting as an expression of our understanding of democracy. 'Enumerative' will be the antonym for all of these terms. 'Enumerative' indicates that we expect there to be a range of choices when it comes to policy decisions or political trajectories all of which will need to be recorded so that in pluralist democracies there is a need to count votes, or similar measures of preference, to get a sense of the majority view *and the range of opinions*—allowing them all to be respected; in contrast, when questions concern matters that are formative there is no point in counting since minority opinions do not have the same legitimacy—they are 'outliers' of one sort or another, not choices that have to be taken into account.

---

[8] For a sociologist the reference might be Durkheim (see note 6).
[9] Which has elsewhere (Collins and Kusch 1998) been related to 'formative action types'.

The Law of Conservation of Democracy

It is the last organic example which is most important for this project. In so far as democracy can only exist so long as citizens want it enough to hold governments to account, the citizens must understand democracy well enough to know what counts as a violation of the culture of democracy. Taking our cue from physics' 'second law of thermodynamics', we'll call this 'the law of conservation of democracy'; it states that democracy can take out only what democracy puts in. Citizens must understand the meaning of democracy and the majority of citizens must actively and continually put that understanding into practice, not least in the way they talk about politics in their day-to-day lives, so reinforcing the idea of democracy through talk and action, if democracy is to last. The over-hasty attempts to convert societies without democratic traditions into instant democracies, and their strong tendency to revert to non-democratic styles of government, often with the tacit or explicit agreement of the citizenry, exemplifies the point. Examples are Sub-Saharan Africa, parts of the former Soviet Union, some Eastern European countries and those countries that experienced the 'Arab Spring'.[10]

We are not arguing that democracy *will necessarily last* if citizens understand it—there are many ways of destroying democracy—we are arguing that *it won't last* if citizens do *not* understand it. Preserving democracies needs citizens who are willing to call to account a government's, or a leader's, non-democratic statements and actions either at elections or via more direct action should democracy break down. We are not here intending to engage in the long running political science debate over whether democracy is best served by increasing the role of the citizenry versus

---

[10] 'The transition from communism has been guided by the principles of legal-rational authority, what I call liberalism and democracy, what I identify as majoritarian selection of the leaders, *Wille der Beherrschten* [the will of those who are governed]. Given the challenges of fast pace of transition, especially of the conversion of public ownership to private wealth, liberal democracy was not consolidated in most—or any?—of these countries. All of these countries—or most of them—are pregnant with a dose of patrimonialism, prebendalism, and illiberalism, and such potentialities come to fruition as long as their charismatic leaders deliver miracles by providing at least the impression of security and improving welfare.' Szelenyi (2016, 23), see also Eyal et al. (2001). For detailed case studies documenting the failure to establish democratic structures across sub-Saharan Africa after 1990, see Diamond and Plattner (2010). Levitsky and Ziblatt (2018, 8) discuss the factors that support democracies at some length. They write 'Democracies work best—and survive longer—where constitutions are reinforced by unwritten democratic norms' (p. 8).

setting pluralist institutions in place: it should be clear that we stress the importance of the right kind of representative institutions, including expert institutions, as opposed to giving ever wider responsibility to citizens. But we do say that the right kind of representative institutions will not be maintained if the people don't know what they want from them. In other words, citizens have to understand, and that means live out, representative, pluralist, democracy if representative, pluralist democracy is to last. There is nothing elitist about citizens choosing to have their elected representatives appoint experts to help them make decisions, as happens with, say the judiciary and the civil service.

Of course, the law of conservation of democracy is in some sense a truism because the argument is that for democracy to survive, democratic 'instincts' must be part of the organic face of society so that the citizens know when something is going wrong; in other words, 'societies must be democratic if democracy is to survive'. But something follows that is not truistic. This is an understanding of how hard it is to create democracies where there is no organic democratic face in the first place: democracies cannot be created simply by changing the procedures used to choose the government. And the 'law' shows that the erosion of a society's existing democratic organic face is likely to lead to the demise of the democracy and this will be hard to reverse. The 'law' tells us we are right to be frightened about what we see happening in today's Western democracies.

The organic, tacit, understanding of what democracy is, establishes the background against which, in democracies, the other type of citizen choice operates; this is the non-organic, enumerated, diverse sets of choices, the aggregates of which are revealed in elections. In elections citizens express their preference for particular policy choices. With this kind of choice there is no expectation that there will be uniformity but that sizeable minorities will express differing opinions on every matter. Pluralist democracies choose to make their decisions according to majority choice, or quasi-majority choice, but do not ignore the minority view. A well-functioning democracy will try to maintain harmony among the disagreeing citizens.

REFERENCES

Collins, Harry. 1985/1992. *Changing Order: Replication and Induction in Scientific Practice*. Chicago: University of Chicago Press. [1992 = second edition]

Collins, Harry. 2018. *Artifictional Intelligence: Against the Humanity's Surrender to Computers*. Cambridge: Polity Press.

Collins, Harry, and Robert Evans. 2017a. *Why Democracies Need Science*. Cambridge and Malden, MA: Polity Press.

———. 2017b. Probes, Surveys, and the Ontology of the Social. *Journal of Mixed Methods Research* 11 (3): 328–341. https://doi.org/10.1177/15586898 15619825.

Collins, Harry M., and Martin Kusch. 1998. *The Shape of Actions: What Humans and Machines Can Do*. Cambridge, MA: MIT Press.

Diamond, Larry, and Marc F. Plattner, eds. 2010. *Democratization in Africa: Progress and Retreat*. Baltimore, MD: Johns Hopkins University Press.

Durant, Darrin. 2011. Models of Democracy in Social Studies of Science. *Social Studies of Science* 41 (5): 691–714.

Durkheim, Émile. 1915. *The Elementary Forms of Religious Life*. Edited by Mark Sydney Cladis and translated by Carol Cosman. Oxford World's Classics. Oxford: Oxford University Press.

———. 2013. *The Division of Labour in Society*. Edited by Steven Lukes and translated by W.D. Halls. Basingstoke: Palgrave Macmillan.

Eyal, Gil, Ivan Szelenyi, and Eleanor R. Townsley. 2001. *Making Capitalism Without Capitalists: The New Ruling Elites in Eastern Europe*. London: Verso.

Levitsky, Steven, and Daniel Ziblatt. 2018. *How Democracies Die*. 1st ed. New York: Crown.

Szelenyi, Ivan. 2016. Weber's Theory of Domination and Post-communist Capitalisms. *Theory and Society* 45: 1–24.

Winch, Peter. 1958. *The Idea of a Social Science and Its Relation to Philosophy*, Studies in Philosophical Psychology. London and New York: Routledge & Kegan Paul.

———. 1964. Understanding a Primitive Society. *American Philosophical Quarterly* 1 (4): 307–324. https://doi.org/10.2307/20009143.

Wittgenstein, Ludwig. 1953. *Philosophical Investigations*. Translated by G.E.M Anscombe. Oxford: Blackwell.

CHAPTER 3

What Is Democracy?

Abstract There are many forms of democracy. Importantly, is there continual accounting to the public via referendums—'direct democracy'—or do the people choose representatives who govern relatively independently between elections? It is natural in representative democracy for experts to be consulted by the elected government, whereas if directness is the ideal, experts can look like unaccountable elites. Under 'pluralist democracy' governments' power is limited by institutional 'checks and balances', such as the judiciary, the free press and alternative parliamentary chambers, ensuring that minorities and minority opinions are not completely suppressed. Checks and balances require experts. There are many other dimensions of democracies including voting systems and the degree of devolution, but an uncritical advocacy of 'rule by the people' is antagonistic to pluralist democracy.

Keywords Democracy • Direct democracy • Representative democracy • Pluralist democracy • Checks and balances • Experts

PREAMBLE

Our purpose in this chapter is to give a brief introduction to democracy for the relatively uninformed reader. Academic volume after academic volume has been dedicated to exploring and evaluating the complexities

© The Author(s) 2020
H. Collins et al., *Experts and the Will of the People*,
https://doi.org/10.1007/978-3-030-26983-8_3

of democracy. For example, Held's, 400 page, *Models of Democracy* has gone through three editions and explores the different forms of democracy in immense detail. Readers who want to understand the full range of what democracy might mean should read a volume of that general kind supported, perhaps, by the references found in our notes. Because of the huge scholarly effort that has been put into analysing democracy one may be sure that any brief voyage into its waters, such as this one, will run aground on someone's favoured analytic island and, without a doubt, a short story like this could be told in many different ways. We simply explain that democracy is complicated and reveal some, if not all, of the dimensions of analytic tension. This sets the scene for later chapters revealing how populism contrasts with every form of pluralist, or moderate, democracy. Those who already understand democracy's complexity should skim-read this chapter, though keeping in mind our definition of 'pluralist democracy' as offered in the Introduction and noting that it excludes strong versions of direct democracy, such as that associated with an ideal communism, where the notion of pluralism is rendered otiose by the theoretical uniformity of the interests of all the people and their government.

Obviously, the entire book turns on a contrast between the subset of democracies, favoured by us—pluralist democracies—and the undesired populism. But this does not mean that every form of democracy is good. Leaders of one-party states and shameless or even murderous tyrannies often refer to their regimes as 'democratic' since the term has a positive valuation and is supposed to indicate that the will of the people is being executed even though it be through a single set of ideas or a single person. To repeat, our term 'pluralist democracy' is meant to maintain a boundary around the subset of systems of government that are favoured here, within the wider group that describe themselves as democratic. Secondly, as has already been intimated, even that subset of pluralist democracies increasingly encounters grotesque and growing inequalities between rich and poor, advantaged and disadvantaged, with the supposed pluralism sometimes being little more than a word. The recent flowering of populism in Western democracies has been explained by the increasingly hopeless prospects for the underclasses. That said, we know where this reaction can lead—to dystopias which make the worst of today's distorted democracies look benign or even, as we saw in the 1930s, to the death of tens of millions of people. In the light of recent happenings, criticism of the post-war

'Western democracies' suddenly seems like a luxury when we need to be defending them against unfolding events. The solution to Western democracy's problems must be a rethinking of the way democracy is regulated so as to alleviate the grotesque inequalities to which it has given rise, not the abandonment of moderation and pluralism in the name of still more 'rule by the people'.

INTRODUCTION

Democracy in its broadest sense involves rule by the many. 'Democracy is an ideal of persons working together in the context of political procedures that treat them as equals ... It conveys an ideal for a political system, one that regulates the formal allocation of political authority'.[1] But what it is to treat people as equals, and what is entailed for a political system, and how that political system regulates political authority, has generated a variety of answers. For example, does treating people as equals mean striving to equalize their opportunities or attempting to make outcomes equal for all? When the political system represents the people, is the people's rule being expressed every few years in elections or should there be a continual stream of votes on every specific issue? Should a democracy strive to allow the people as much direct and continuous influence on the process of government or a more indirect power over a set of decision-making representatives or institutions?[2] In turn, there are many ways of executing each of these choices.

---

[1] Waldron (2012, 187).

[2] Held in his 1995 book sub-divides the choice into three: "direct or participatory democracy", "liberal or representative democracy", and "one-party" democracy but since the latter is hardly democracy at all, the basic choice is that between direct and indirect. One-party democracies might go by names such as 'The People's Democratic Republic of X' exemplified by, say, China, North Korea, Vietnam, Yemen and Ethiopia. Quite a few such nations are characterised by human rights violations, control or suppression of the press, and a police and/or judiciary under the thrall of the state so that political pluralism is a sham at best; one party 'democracies' are breaching experiments which indicate some of the essential features of what we are calling pluralist democracy. Held elsewhere distinguishes between participatory democracy, which can be pluralist, and direct democracy, which is not. Direct democracy would be something like full-blown communism in which ideal egalitarianism leads to the identity of interests of every citizen and the state so pluralism is otiose. But, as already mentioned, while this might be admirable as an ideal it seems that nation-scale experiments suggest that such regimes are rarely desirable in practice.

THE CITY STATE

The term democracy comes from the Greek *demokratia demos* (people) and *kratos* (rule), and sixth century BC Athens is generally taken as the model. In Athens the power of the ruling (wealthy) families was shifted towards the citizens by allowing them to participate in deliberations and vote on decisions. Athens, however, placed restriction on who counted as a citizen.[3] Women, slaves and foreigners could not vote, which probably excluded about three-quarters of the population. Second, citizen power increased with wealth; the wealthier were entitled to sit on decision-making assemblies with wider powers that wielded authority over more numerous or more important social domains.

Greece also had a word for the feared excesses of democracy—too much 'people power': this was *ochlocracy*, or 'mob rule'. Mob rule meant emotional, self-interested and possibly prejudiced citizens bringing instability and rashness to public decision-making. For Plato democracy was constantly flirting with instability, because the voting *demos* (the people) were always vulnerable to descending into a mad crowd. For Plato, the solution involved selecting rulers according to their skills, especially the skill of statecraft. Aristotle was more impressed by the idea of the people's voice moderating the threat of tyranny and so he suggested rulers should be selected according to their degree of virtue. Thus we can see the tension over unrestricted people power already moderating the ideal of democracy, people power becoming filtered and complemented by the deliberations of selected groups of representatives. Of course, Plato's notorious 'philosopher kings' have become an icon for fascism given that they were supposed to be able to know the desires of the people better than the people themselves. There are no easy solutions to the enigmas of democracy.[4]

In Athens citizen participation was immediate and citizens expressed their will via institutions in which they were physically present—a literal 'directness'. In more current discussions of democracy, 'directness' is better understood as 'unmediated by others', with the crucial questions concerning how to understand and know the true preferences of citizens. The principle of direct democracy is most famously defended by Jean-Jacques Rousseau (1712–1778), who wrote that:

---

[3] Osborne (2012, 7–28).
[4] Dahl (1956, 33–37) offers various formulations of what democracy means.

sovereignty *cannot be represented* for the same reason that it cannot be alien-ated. It consists essentially in the general will, and the will cannot be repre-sented; it is either itself or something else; no middle ground is possible. The deputies of the people, therefore, neither are nor can be its representatives; they are nothing other than its commissaries; they cannot conclude anything definitively (our emphasis).[5]

Rousseau's conception of popular sovereignty is, then, synonymous with the will of the people. Sovereignty cannot be delegated to others, for sovereignty conceived of as the will of the people, emanating directly from the people, is no longer legitimate once it is represented by another.[6]

The role of elections is another way to think about the nature of democ-racies and the choices that have to be made within them. The election of representatives can be said to take power away from the people.[7] Under Rousseau's conception, sovereignty is undermined by representation and the route to populism is laid down: any time the government spends away from the direct voices of citizens is a dangerous time. For Rousseau liberty can only mean direct self-rule which, as far as elections are concerned, would imply continual referenda.

REPRESENTATIVE/LIBERAL DEMOCRACY

How do large collectives of people balance self-rule with the need for coercive institutions such as the criminal justice system and institutions that create laws? Representative democracy and its close cousin liberal democracy favour more indirect forms of political representation, enacted through independent institutions along with the protection of rights: citi-zens vote for legislators to represent them. Unfortunately, the story of liberal democracy can be told as either the steady expansion of the fran-chise or as the steady collapse of democratic politics into mere electioneering.[8] An in-between model known as 'deliberative democracy'

---

[5] Rousseau (1987 [1762], 198).
[6] See Urbinati (2006a, 60–100) for the best treatment of Rousseau's justification for direct democracy.
[7] Sartori (1965, 108).
[8] For Turner (2003), it appears the answer is that liberal democracy has moved on to a stage where the franchise is complicated by information asymmetries between experts and non-experts and the solution that has been adopted amounts to a makeshift pragmatic move to house debates in commissions of enquiry. Turner calls the stages Liberal Democracy 1.0

prefers the framing of laws to involve extensive deliberation by legislators and sections of the public.[9] Different versions of deliberative democracy turn on the extent to which citizens are involved in the deliberating process and what role citizens play in determining policy outcomes. In one variant it is a moderating influence on representative democracy with a legitimate role for experts.[10] In deliberative democracy, representatives are never alone with their judgments but always facing the permanent (even if only in potential) attention and contestation of citizens.[11] What we have called pluralist democracies may well include some larger or smaller element of deliberation which can provide additional forums, over and above their role in advising governments, in which expert consultants might interact and even learn.

WHO ARE THE PEOPLE AND HOW OFTEN DO THEY VOTE?

Of particular concern for this book, given our focus on expertise and science, are the assumptions made about the capacities of citizens under direct and indirect models of democracy. To start with direct democracy, the assumption appears to be that all citizens are able to form meaningful opinions about any and all of the issues on which they are to be consulted. In the agora of Ancient Greece, and perhaps even in eighteenth Century France, this may have been a reasonable assumption. For contemporary

democracy that is actually just rule by notables), 2.0 (democracy by recognition and inclusion) and 3.0 (democracy by delegation to commissions and bureaucracies).

[9] See Habermas (1996) and Rawls (1993).

[10] Pitkin (1967, 209). Habermas (1996) is the most notable theorists in this regard. Habermas posits an ideal speech situation that underpins our communicative exchanges: citizens actively engage in deliberation via their ethical-political discourses, enabling them to agree despite differences.

[11] Urbinati (2006b, 25, 27). Both Turner (2003) in his discussion of liberal democracy and Urbinati (2006a) in her discussion of representational democracy share the idea that both forms of democracy depend on vibrant discussion, beyond electoral competition, in order for the conditions of legitimate decision-making to persist. How vibrant the discussion should be is a matter of dispute, with 'radical democracy' theorists emphasizing the role conflict and identity differences play in redressing marginalization and ensuring the autonomy of minorities by stressing that they must be respected. Theorists like Mouffe (2000) charge that Habermas over-emphasizes consensus-seeking behaviour and under-appreciates the role conflict or agonistic relations play in addressing marginalization and inequality in our democracies. Taylor (1998) argues in a like-minded vein, but stresses the way "people can bond together in difference without abstracting from their differences" (p. 153) to highlight the role the preservation of group-based differences plays in sustaining citizen autonomy.

societies, however, with their complex divisions of highly specialised labour, proliferation of interest groups and identities, and sheer number of issues and problems, the assumption of omni-competence seems implausible, even fantastical. It is no longer possible, if it ever was, for anyone to be an expert in everything. As the journalist and political commentator Walter Lippman wrote almost 100 years ago in his classic text *The Phantom Public*:

> The individual man does not have opinions on all public affairs. He does not know how to direct public affairs. He does not know what is happening, why it is happening, what ought to happen. I cannot imagine how he could know, and there is not the least reason for thinking, as mystical democrats have thought, that the compounding of individual ignorances in masses of people can continue directing force in public affairs.[12]

There are two problems here. First, there is the sheer volume of information that needs to be processed. Second, and linked to this, most of the sources that citizens will use to gather information and form their views will have already filtered, interpreted and re-presented the primary information.[13]

The conclusion Lippmann draws from this is that experts have an important role to play in any democratic society, with the job of representative government being to develop the expertise needed to select experts and hold them to account; citizens are then responsible for holding the legislators to account in their management of the experts. This way of framing the relationship between experts, elected officials, and the general public, recognises that experts inevitably have some autonomy as a result of their expertise. As a result, Lippman's attempt to recognise the inevitable asymmetries of knowledge in industrial societies has been read by many as anti-democratic! This resonates with more recent debates in the social studies of science about the ability of lay citizens to make technical judgements.

For proponents of direct democracy, and of civic capacity in general, a more congenial model of the public comes from the work of philosopher John Dewey, that was published at the same time as Lippmann's work and is often seen as a critique of it. For Dewey, the public is not to be under-

---

[12] Quote at p. 29 of Lippmann (1993, 10); for a more contemporary take, see Warren (1996).

[13] Lippmann (2007).

stood as every citizen but only those engaged by a controversy. Issues thus create *publics* and this, in turn, solves some of the problems identified by Lippmann. An 'issue-public' of the kind described by Dewey is much like a modern-day pressure group or social movement. Its members are motivated to become knowledgeable and are able to engage with experts in a sophisticated way. Citizens of this kind are meant to have gained competence in a circumscribed domain and be able to make judgements about the quality and application of expert advice for themselves and without the need for intermediary institutions.[14]

Although the so-called 'debate' between Lippmann and Dewey is often seen as being about the critique of democracy by Lippman and its defence by Dewey, we prefer to see it as a disagreement about the capacities of citizens and how these can best be used. Both make good points but, because they rely on different examples they are talking about different things. Lippmann's problem is how every ordinary citizen can comprehend the full-range of contested information implied in the issues that matter in democratic societies—economics, defence, health, technology, education, international relations, and so on—and his conclusion is that they cannot, and that democratic societies need some institutional mechanism through which this scrutiny is carried out. Citizens, and elected officials, are then charged with selecting experts and judging their work. In contrast, Dewey is concerned with the capacity of individuals or narrow groups of citizens to engage with and challenge experts. In this case, there is no assumption that all citizens can or need to engage in this way. Rather, the important point is that some can, and these should be enabled to do so in order to ensure effective scrutiny and improve the quality of decisions. Given the intensity of training and socialisation of technical experts the debate about the depth and effectiveness of citizen expertise won't go away and vaccination revolts are, as so often, an object lesson in how problems can arise.

This tension between breadth and depth of civic engagement in democratic politics is at the heart of debates about the merits of different approaches to democracy. If neither extreme of direct nor indirect democracy is viable in the long run, how then can citizens be enabled to participate most effectively in democratic institutions? Representative democracies can include and encourage deliberation within and between citizens in many ways. The most basic is simply through civic education and the execution of a citizen's duty. Simply by living within a democratic society

---

[14] Dewey (1954 [1927]) and Marres (2007). For case studies illustrating the point, see for example Epstein (1996), Irwin (1995), Geffen (2010) and Ottinger (2013).

and upholding its values, citizens perform a vital role in maintaining the values and institutions of that society. This contribution is typically unnoticed, like water goes unnoticed by a fish, but every time a citizen acknowledges the rights of others to hold or express views that differ from their own, or to make choices that they would not make themselves, they reaffirm that they and their peers are free and equal before the law. More formal ways of making such a contribution include: voting at general elections; taking part in referenda—frequent in some countries, rare in others; responding to opinion polls or more deliberative forms of polling; taking part in consensus conferences or citizen juries and working with expert committees; there can be much more to democracy than voting.[15]

FORMS OF DEMOCRACY

Let us list some of the choices that are involved in the formation of democracies. A democracy is made up of many components. There are the people, there are rights, there is voting, there is a government, there is separation of powers and there are other kinds of checks and balances. The notion of 'rule by the people' allows for an almost endless multiplicity of *democracies* depending on how these components are conceived and how they act and are acted upon. We have seen some of the possibilities in some of the main types of democracy described above. Here we will try to put some of the components of democracy together, listing the different choices that democracies have available to them. Some of these combinations would not add up to pluralist democracy but what we are looking to do here is approach exhaustiveness. The touchstone of pluralist democracies is moderation so they will lean toward choices which safeguard minorities, allow a normal opposition, favour more than one parliamentary chamber and, as we will argue in this book, allow plenty of scope for the elected government to make use of experts.

- *The people*: Are the people treated as an organic group or is the people's view seen as a matter of enumerating opinions and interests with a majority and various minorities that will be treated in such a way that the majority will not dominate everything? How closely coupled are the public and the government; is the public seen as always sovereign

---

[15] For a detailed analysis of the British Colombia Citizens' Assembly, a bold experiment in deliberative democracy, and its implications for democratic theory, see Warren and Pearse (2008).

or a body that chooses representatives? Is there an in-between situation—deliberative democracy—in which citizens are brought into dialogue with the elected members of a representative democracy? Are the public really a set of publics with different interests based on locality, identity, gender, ethnicity, class and/or income? Are there publics with different sets of expertises who might be thought to bring more or less valuable opinions to the deliberative aspects of democracy?

- *Rights*: Is there a right to equality of treatment and does this mean equality of opportunity or equality of outcome? How far does the right to express unusual, offensive or inciteful views extend to the tolerance of intolerance? How far does it extend to the right to complete economic freedom without state intervention to limit economic inequality or the pathologies of unconstrained markets? How far does it extend to the right to own dangerous weapons or dangerous substances, animals or other organisms and the right to endanger or infect others? How far does it extend to the right to refuse health treatments for oneself or family members, especially when this affects the population as a whole (as in the case of vaccination)?

- *Voting*: How often does the population vote for new leaders or representatives? How universal is the franchise? Does the electorate vote as a single body or is it divided into constituencies, or states, or cantons, or similar? Is the ruling party that with the most votes or that with the most elected representatives of sub-divisions of the electorate? Is the strength of opposition parties decided by number of representatives elected (which tends to minimise their strength and number), or by the number of votes for each party ('first past the post' versus proportional representation)?

- *The government*: Is there a single ruling party (more likely in the case of first past the post) or a leading party supported by a coalition of other parties (more likely with proportional representation)? What proportion of decision-making applies to the nation as a whole and what proportion is distributed to elements within a federal system? Who decides when it is time for a new election and how is it decided? How are party-members controlled and what is the role of the opposition parties? How strongly is the government controlled by a written constitution and how is the constitution changed? What is the role and the influence of wealthy interest groups?[16]

---

[16] Many of these distinctions are discussed in Lijphart (1999, 2012).

- *Separation of powers and checks and balances*: How many chambers are there making up the government, what are their respective powers and to what extent can they limit the power of the other branches of government? Is there a president, elected separately from the members of government, or a prime minister who leads elected representatives with the consent of a political party, and is merely first among equals? How do the elected leaders work with the professional administration? How free are the press and other media, universities and schools, and the other producers of influential cultural output? How independent is the central bank? And, the focus of this book, how free are scientific experts to work independently and make their views widely known; to what extent is the government bound to take these views into account?

As we will see in the next chapter, certain sets of these choices remove restrictions on the power of government such as by weakening checks and balances resulting in a 'democracy' that is close to or identical to populism.

REFERENCES

Dahl, Robert. 1956. *A Preface to Democratic Theory*. Chicago: University of Chicago Press.

Dewey, John. 1954 [1927]. *The Public and its Problems*. Athens, OH: Swallow Press. (Original work published 1927.)

Epstein, Steven. 1996. *Impure Science: AIDS, Activism, and the Politics of Knowledge*. Berkeley: University of California Press.

Geffen, Nathan. 2010. *Debunking Delusions: The Inside Story of the Treatment Action Campaign*. Johannesburg: Jacana Media.

Habermas, Jürgen. 1996. *Between Facts and Norms: Contributions to a Discourse Theory of Law and Democracy*. Translated by William Rehg. Cambridge, MA: MIT Press.

Held, David. 1995. *Democracy and the Global Order: From the Modern State to Cosmopolitan Governance*. Stanford, CA: Stanford University Press.

Irwin, Alan. 1995. *Citizen Science: A Study of People, Expertise, and Sustainable Development*, Environment and Society. London and New York: Routledge.

Lijphart, Arend. 1999. *Patterns of Democracy: Government Forms and Performance in Thirty-Six Countries*. New Haven, CT: Yale University Press.

———. 2012. *Patterns of Democracy: Government Forms and Performance in Thirty-Six Countries*. 2nd updated and expanded ed. New Haven, CT: Yale University Press.

Lippmann, Walter. 1993. *The Phantom Public*. New Brunswick, NJ: Transaction Publishers.

———. 2007. *Public Opinion*. La Vergne, TN: BN Publishing.

Marres, Noortje. 2007. The Issues Deserve More Credit: A Pragmatist Contribution to the Study of Public Involvement in Controversy. *Social Studies of Science* 37 (5): 759–780.

Mouffe, Chantal. 2000. *The Democratic Paradox*. London: Verso.

Osborne, Roger. 2012. *Of the People, by the People: A New History of Democracy*. London: Pimlico.

Ottinger, Gwen. 2013. *Refining Expertise: How Responsible Engineers Subvert Environmental Justice Challenges*. New York: New York University Press.

Pitkin, Hanna Fenichel. 1967. *The Concept of Representation*. Berkeley: University of California Press.

Rawls, John. 1993. *Political Liberalism*. Expanded ed. Columbia Classics in Philosophy. New York: Columbia University Press.

Rousseau, Jean-Jacques. 1987 [1762]. On the Social Contract, or Principles of Political Rights. In *Basic Political Writings*, trans. and ed. Donald A. Cres, 139–227. Indianapolis, IN: Hackett.

Sartori, Giovanni. 1965. *Democratic Theory*. New York: Praeger.

Taylor, Charles. 1998. The Dynamic of Democratic Exclusion. *Journal of Democracy* 9 (4): 143–156.

Turner, Stephen P. 2003. *Liberal Democracy 3.0: Civil Society in an Age of Experts*, Theory, Culture & Society. London and Thousand Oaks, CA: SAGE Publications.

Urbinati, Nadia. 2006a. *Representative Democracy: Principles and Genealogy*. Chicago: University of Chicago Press.

———. 2006b. Political Representation as a Democratic Process. Edited by K Palonen. *Redescriptions—Yearbook of Political Thought and Conceptual History* 10 (1): 18–40.

Waldron, J. 2012. Democracy. In *The Oxford Handbook of Political Philosophy*, ed. David Estlund, 197–203. Oxford: Oxford University Press.

Warren, Mark. 1996. What Should We Expect from More Democracy?: Radically Democratic Responses to Politics. *Political Theory* 24 (2): 241–270.

Warren, Mark, and Hilary Pearse, eds. 2008. *Designing Deliberative Democracy: The British Columbia Citizens' Assembly*. Cambridge and New York: Cambridge University Press.

CHAPTER 4

What Is Populism?

Abstract Populism contrasts clearly with pluralist democracy. By treating the result of elections as representing 'the will of the people', populism misrepresents the enumerative face of society as the organic face and defines all opposition to the elected government as traitorous. Minorities, and the institutions and experts upon which the checks and balance of pluralist democracy depend, are, therefore, attacked by populist leaders. Populist leaders claim that their actions, however dictatorial, and however much they favour a specific group in society, are democratic—they represent the will of the people. Because populism, in its championing of the people, is anti-elitist, some commentators consider it can enliven democracy. In today's world, however, the dangers are obvious: attacks on minorities and the control of what counts as expertise.

Keywords Populism • Pluralist democracy • Organic and enumerative faces of society • Checks and balances • The will of the people

IDEAL-TYPE *POPULISM*

Here we explain populism drawing on the account of society offered in Chap. 2. We explain the way it can be confused with democracy drawing on the account of democracy in Chap. 3. Populism has a strange relationship with democracy since it is often said to be in tension with it, but both are described as government 'according to the will of the people'. Populism

© The Author(s) 2020   35
H. Collins et al., *Experts and the Will of the People*,
https://doi.org/10.1007/978-3-030-26983-8_4

has been described as the 'permanent shadow' of representative politics.[1] The shadowy nature is made possible by the variety of types of democracy and an enthusiasm to give direct power to the people rather than their representatives; the more direct the democracy the nearer it comes to populism and there are theorists who believe that populist politics and populist ideas invigorate democracy.[2] We will explain why some who favour democracy are also attracted to populism in a section below entitled 'But populism can be confused with democracy'. First, though, we can set out clear differences and dangers by comparing democracy with a certain 'ideal type' of populism. We develop our understanding of this ideal type by starting with Jan-Werner Müller's account in his, *What is populism?*

There are many variants of populism, some of which are well-intentioned, being essentially anti-elitist and seeing themselves as supporting the people against corrupt leadership. This is sometimes known as left-wing populism. The extent to which left-wing populism is subject to the same critique as we mount here against populism in general is a matter of the extent to which it works against pluralism and moderation. We will pay some attention to less extreme versions of populism by subtracting this or that feature of the ideal type as some of these variants are attractive due to the way they approach more benign variants of democracy in intention, irrespective of outcome. For the sake of exposition, from here on we'll use the italicised '*populism*' to stand for the ideal, right-wing, type along with such left wing variants as are antagonistic to pluralism.[3]

All the time we have in mind that too much enthusiasm for safeguarding rule by the people leads toward populism and a benign populism is hard to maintain; in this book we are, of course, especially concerned with

---

[1] See Müller (2017).

[2] See Arditi (2003), Mouffe (2000), Laclau (2005).

[3] An ideal type is a sociological concept used to refer to an imagined composite version of something that contains all the characteristics one might hope to find in a real case. Other analysts of populism such as Mudde and Kaltwasser (2017), might emphasise different contrasts—for example that populism is essentially anti-elitist. We are stressing that it is essentially anti-pluralist, though it might be anti-elitist too in some incarnations. There are also differences between left-wing and right-wing populists (Judis 2016). Mouffe (2018) is an example of the kind of left-wing populist who, nevertheless, sustains a commitment to pluralism but she fails to explain the role of expert knowledge. Laclau (2005) too claims there are such an immense variety of populisms that it pays to focus on populism *conceptually* rather than chase each variant so as to list all the divergent content of populisms in any given instance. Our ideal type is taken from Müller (2017) but additional points are developed based on that book's basic logic.

the role of experts and, especially scientific experts, as a vital element in the distribution of power in democracies and a safeguard against populist drift. This means, among other things, that we will declare a preference for the kinds of democracies—pluralist democracies—where there is a clear space for experts over those where experts might be seen as irrelevant or dangerous. The strong form of *populism*, as well as being easy to contrast with pluralist democracy, is important because many commentators see, in recent events, a revival, or potential revival of extreme ideas that threaten democratic societies; some certainly think the current state of affairs has echoes of the 1930's precursors of fascism.[4]

POPULISM AND DEMOCRACY

One crucial difference between *populism* and pluralist democracy is that in the second what the people want is regularly tested by elections (more or less frequently under different variants). Furthermore, as explained in the Introduction, the choice of the people is normally ascertained in democracy by counting votes in the regular elections and the outcome is thought of as *enumerative*, with a range of opinions, majority and minority, recorded; the outcome of such vote-counting is not thought of as organic or *constitutive*. The choice of the people is understood to be pluralistic under pluralist democracy and, therefore, as explained in the Introduction, the power of the majority expressed through voting needs to be moderated by checks and balances such as the party system which filters the kind of candidates that can be elected for office, the recognition of the role of the opposition parties leaving open the possibility that a government can be unseated by a revolt of a smallish number of its own MPs, bicameral systems and the like, and separation of powers such as in an independent legal system and a free press. The crucial feature of *populism*, in contrast, is that it takes the enumerated, usually majority, choice of the people to be *the will of the people* (the phrase will be italicised when referring to the *populist* version), not as diverse but as having an ontological unity representing the 'real people'—'real Hungarians', 'real Americans'—who embody the national will and can be contrasted to the minorities who only pretend to be 'real citizens' so as to usurp their rights. The majority choice is treated as *constitutive* rather than something that should be expected to

---

[4]See for example Douthat (2018), Mudde (2017, 2018), World Forum for Democracy (2017), Roth (2017).

change at the next election or succeeding ones, as would be the case if the result were understood to be enumerative and treated under a pluralist philosophy; instead, change is thought of as betrayal and is best prevented. Under both *populism* and pluralist democracy, the new government is elected by the 'majority' but, under populism, the 'majority' outcome of the vote becomes defined as the will of all the people with the views of those who disagree being subject to processes that tend to make them disappear from view. Worse, the upholders of minority views will come to be defined not, as in the British phrase, 'the loyal opposition', but as positively disloyal for opposing '*the will of the people*'.[5] Under *populism*, this metaphysical *will of the people* (hereafter sometimes written as '*the will*' or simply '*will*') is mobilised by the elected representatives who use various persuasive means to make *the will* still more attractive to the sector that elected them and more readily accepted by others as embodying the organic *will*. Under this model, any separation of powers can only weaken the expression of the metaphysical *will* so it is morally justified to degrade the independence of the legal system and the freedom of the press and eliminate parliamentary checks and balances: removing these constraints on *the will* is, in turn, described as being desired by the people so as to make *the will* of the true people stronger, purer and easier to execute. A growing proportion of the people probably do come to want all this and more as the persuasive machinery of the new leaders takes effect. There is, then, a recognisable route from populism to a dictatorship, or fascism. Nevertheless, it can be claimed that a concentration of power is democratically justified since the dictator is doing nothing more than enacting *the will of the people*.[6] We see, then, that two transmutations take place

---

[5] 'Majority' is in scare-quotes because under certain electoral systems the winners might not actually have the major share of the popular vote, as they did not in the case of the election of President Trump in the USA. Weale (2018), points out that what 'majority' means is very unclear: first we have to take into account who is allowed to vote; second we have to take into account that not everybody who can vote does vote. This means that the proportion of the people who make up a 'majority' in an election and are taken to be expressing the 'will of the people' with their votes can be quite small. Weale points out that the number of voters who actually vote in Swiss referendums is about 50% of those entitled from which it follows that in a close run decision the number of people making the decision will be less than a quarter of the Swiss people. Weale also points out that people are often asked to vote for coalitions that stand for all manner of cross-cutting policies so under these circumstances what even this minority of people really want *cannot* be expressed by their voting.

[6] As Hitler put it in a speech of 1935: '*Ein Volk*, Ein Reich, Ein Führer' [One People, One Empire, One Leader]. Or, a still clearer expression in a speech by Goebbels: "The nation and

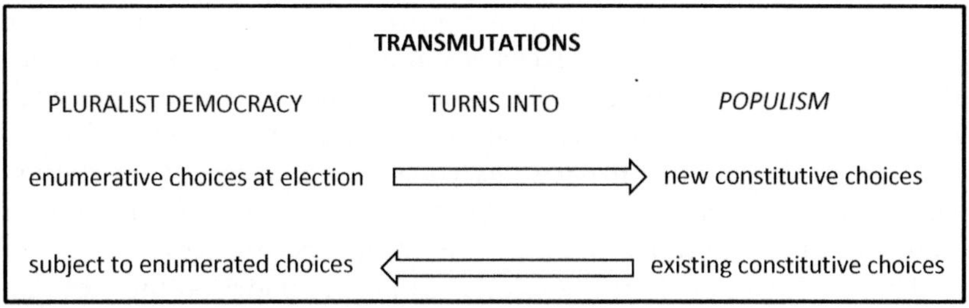

Fig. 4.1 Transmutations

when we shift from pluralist democracy to *populism*: an enumerated electoral choice is transmuted into a constitutive choice while past constitutive choices are treated as subject to change as a result of the new election. For example, the electoral victory of a party that is prejudiced against an ethnic minority and claims to understand the true *will of the people* leads to the redefinition of citizenship, an essentially constitutive matter, to exclude the ethnic minority (see Fig. 4.1).[7]

BUT POPULISM CAN BE CONFUSED WITH DEMOCRACY

Some analysts have claimed that there are three main elements to populism: anti-elitism, anti-pluralism, and an adulation of the common people.[8] If we ignore the anti-pluralism, the remaining two features hold the people's power in opposition to distant elites and their cold ways. One can see how attractive this aspect of populism is to those who hold a model of democracy in which the most important thing is for the people to hold sway over elites, including scientific elites. We can see that some analysts would say that this aspect of populism bolsters democracy rather than

the government in Germany are one thing. The Will of the people is the Will of the government and vice versa. The modern structure of the German State is a higher form of democracy in which, by virtue of the people's mandate, the government is exercised authoritatively while there is no possibility for parliamentary interference, to obliterate and render ineffective the execution of the nation's Will." Josef Goebbels "On National-Socialist Germany And Her Contribution Towards Peace." Speech to the representatives of the international press at Geneva on September 28, 1933. German League of Nations Union News Service, PRO, FO 371/16728.

[7] For a different kind of criticism of the meaning of 'the will of the people', see Weale (2018) and note 35.

[8] Müller (2017) and Mudde and Kaltwasser (2017).

opposing it. If it is thought that elite processes fatally limit the scope of political action for ordinary citizens or various kinds of social movements, the claim can seem reasonable. The trouble is that you cannot take away the anti-pluralism and still have populism. So anti-elitism cannot afford to take comfort from populism if it wants to maintain pluralism. Pluralistically-motivated anti-elitism must still support those elites that are an essential feature of the division of powers and the checks and balances.

The view that populism is good for democracy trades on the idea that popular sovereignty and the representational/liberal dimensions of democracy are incompatible.[9] Those stressing the incompatibility between the people's democracy and liberal democracy hold the institutions belonging to the latter to be not truly representative of the people. The combination of checks and balances and distant and out-of-touch institutions and elected representatives is thought to undermine the ability of the people to be seen, heard and included. Populism is thought to be continuous with democracy because the emphasis is upon reconnecting people directly to deliberative and decision-making powers. The argument makes complete sense in the light of Rousseau's idea that citizens renounce their sovereignty as soon as they consent to be represented.[10]

WE HAVE ALWAYS BEEN POPULISTS

Some of the actions and statements of political actors who inhabit what are, for the moment, pluralist democracies, have dangerous, implicit, and presumably overlooked, populist connotations and consequences. In Britain we see this in the aftermath of the Brexit vote where certain politicians proclaim that it is impossible to go back on the vote because it embodies something even these avowed democrats call *the will of the people* (it seems appropriate to italicise it even though at least some of the users are, probably, not self-conscious populists); this metaphysical entity, they say, has been expressed, once and for all, in the referendum. In this respect, the will of the people of the United Kingdom is being taken to have ontological unity even though 48 per cent of those who voted—those who voted being only 72% of those eligible to vote—and the majority of the

---

[9] Chantal Mouffe (2000) refers to this incompatibility as the democratic paradox.

[10] The best treatment of Rousseau's conception of the relationship between sovereignty and representation is Urbinati (2006a, b). In Urbinati (2006a) see her chap. 2 'Rousseau's Unrepresentable Sovereign'.

voters in Scotland and Northern Ireland—two of the UK's four constituent nations—were of the opposite view. The will of the people is here being used as a metaphysical gag on debate about the wisdom of the Brexit decision. It is being said by fervent supporters of the government, that this will having shown itself once, cannot be questioned and the vote cannot be repeated.[11] The situation in Britain at the start of 2018 has been described as a failure of democracy:

> This is what a democratic deficit looks like. There is a gap in our politics where full-throated opposition to the madness of Brexit should be. Easy to forget amid solemn invocations of "the will of the people", but 49% of Britons [it should be voters] voted to remain. So it is left to a party with just 12 MPs, along with the SNP, to speak for them.[12]

Again, this situation was prefigured in social studies of science in an analysis of the American election of the year 2000. In an article with the main title 'What is TWAP', it was pointed out that what was being widely referred to as *the will of the American people (TWAP)* had emerged from a vote where the difference between one side and the other was within the 'noise' of the electoral process so *the will* arose at random but was then treated as an ontological reality that legitimated the new regime in spite of its origins in chance occurrences.[13] This kind of invocation gives strength to those who want to argue that nothing new is being witnessed in the contemporary scene—that, as it were, 'we have always been populists'. This section of the chapter has shown one of the ways that some

---

[11] See Howard Jacobson's (2017) critique of Tory politician Jacob Rees-Mogg who has invoked *the will of the people* in the populist sense on numerous occasions. Note that the Brexit choice is one of those cases, like vaccination (first discussed in the Introduction), where one cannot allow a subset of the population not to Brexit while everyone else does, however pluralist one would like to be. But, also like vaccination, it is a case where consideration for the minority would allow for the possibility of reversal of the decision if deeper understanding develops; exactly what the will of the people rhetoric as the Brexit argument unfolded was designed to avoid.

[12] Freedland (2018).

[13] See Collins et al. (2001). The problem was given special salience in this election because votes in some states were counted by machines reading punch cards. Unfortunately, the machines in the voting booths did not always punch a clean hole, which meant that these votes were not included in the count. As the margin of victory was so small, this lead to a controversy about what to do with cards in which the 'hanging chad' meant they were not counted automatically but from which some indication of the voter's intention could be derived.

liberal-minded people can believe that nothing new or unusual is happening with recent political events: certain critiques of democracy have an overlap with the same anti-elitist sentiments at the forefront of the creature that is populism; but the creature is a Trojan horse.

PROUDLY VIOLATING DEMOCRACY

To return to *populism* proper, complete with anti-pluralism, it has one very important feature that must be understood if certain actions that tend in that direction are to be distinguished from certain very similar actions that are found in pluralist democracies; we put more emphasis on this feature than Müller.[14] Examples of these actions include limiting and distorting the powers of the courts or the press or failing to tell the truth to the citizenry. The important thing is that when these things happen under pluralist democracy they are concealed as they are a cause for shame and, if exposed, might lead to the removal of governments by a revolt of MPs, or impeachment, or its equivalent. Under *populism*, however, such actions are taken to be legitimate on the grounds that they are necessary if *the will of the people* is to be expressed and actualised in an unhampered way. In order to legitimate them the actions are not hidden but proudly proclaimed and exhibited. The public display of what would normally be taken to be violations of democracy leads to their legitimation; *the will*, as expressed by the rulers, is shown to create what counts as the truth itself. The iconic incident is Trump's claim that the crowd at his election address was larger than that for Obama along with his spokesperson, Kellyanne Conway's, claim that this was an 'alternative fact'. This should not be read as a misplaced remark by a stupid person, but part of an attempt to realign the meaning of truth with the 'emotional truths' that the newly elected representatives of the people found most convenient; it should be seen as part of an attempt to relocate the locus of truth from the traditional expert community to the governing elite and an attempt to engineer a collapse of the separation of powers between the two.[15] That is the difference between what is happen-

---

[14] Müller does mention it several times in his opening chapters but does not include it among his final summary of characteristics.

[15] Temelkuran (2019), explicitly draws connections between the normalisation of shamelessness, alternative facts, and the democratic peril detaching specialist knowledge from democratic institutions. These are all parts of the 'steps', he says, from democracy to dictatorship. As the year 2017 unfolded, it became clear that lying was an integral part of 'Trumpism'. See Leonard and Thompson (2017) for an extensive list of Trump's lies in 2017 and the

ing now and the many, many lies, including lies about technical issues, that have been told by non-populist democratic politicians through the decades: the democratic politicians tacitly accepted that lying was wrong and tried to hide the shameful actions whereas Trump and Conway's strategy is proud proclamation of the violations in the hope that they will cease to be seen as violations but, rather, a legitimate feature of strong government.

Under pluralist democracy the very concealment of what normally counts as violations of democracy reinforces the basic values of democracy; under *populism*, the public displays of what would once have been counted as violations shows that they are no longer to be counted violations; these public displays are, therefore, attacks on the basic values of democratic society proper.[16]

The reason that this feature of populism is particularly important in a discussion of its relation to science is that in recent years, in academic fields such as science studies, media studies and political science, one could frequently hear the cynical comment that nothing new was happening and that politicians had always lied and cheated and tried to corrupt the courts and so on.[17] Our own academic world of social studies of science, and we do not know if this reflects a more widespread situation, is split into two camps, those like the authors of this book who think we are presented with a potentially terrifying political problem for the Western democracies, which could be paving the way for dystopia or even a repeat of the events of the 1930s, and those who think that what we are seeing is simply a continuation of the typical corruption of democracies. But the nothing-new-here position overlooks the shameless, proud, presentation of the violation of democratic values that is found in populism, changing it from the normal corruption found in democracy into an attack on democracy's basic values.[18]

Washington Post archive https://www.washingtonpost.com/news/fact-checker/wp/category/donald-trump/.

[16] 'Hypocrisy is the homage that vice pays to virtue' (François de La Rochefoucauld); nowadays, even hypocrisy is being abandoned. On the way the politics of political correctness has evolved, see Sparrow (2018).

[17] See for example, the recent series of articles on the relationship between STS and what has been called 'post-truth' which are referenced in note 16 in Chap. 5. For an example of how to admit lying and bullshit and fabricated silences have always been part of politics including the politics of science, but not suggest what we are seeing is more of the same, see Keane (2018). Keane notes, among other things, the way digital media penetrate the public/private boundary so easily, effectively colonizing daily life.

[18] For an example of political scientists who see the relationship between today's events and the 1930s, see Levitsky and Ziblatt (2018).

Another feature that makes the Twenty-First Century version of populism even more volatile than that of the 1930s is mass media and social media. There are far more television and radio channels while social media platforms carry information, opinion, claim and counter-claim into every corner of social life. The line between fantasy and reality is blurred. Entertainment and advertising are no longer distinct. While in the digital age the potential for citizens to acquire information has exploded, the passive recipient has no means to separate the valuable from the tendentious or false. Even policy-makers can 'become captive to their own fictions'—the echo chambers and 'filter bubbles' of our digital age contributing to a political life 'insulated from any reality check'.[19] All this feeds into the processes by which a majority can become a self-affirming 'people'. An increasingly vital element of 'civic education' is education about the role of the internet and its potential, especially in the hands of those with malicious intent— that is those who want to disrupt the ability of the public to make choices based on deliberative understanding and to disrupt civic education itself.

POPULISM SUMMARISED

There is a superficial political sympathy between direct kinds of democracy and certain features of populism but we need to know what is to be avoided if we are to preserve pluralist democracy and avoid a possibly well-intentioned endorsement of movements that we don't fully understand. The following is a list of the characteristics of a strong populism and of these we should be wary[20]:

1. *The will of the people*, even if initially indicated by an election, is seen as organic, unitary and constitutive of society; it is not seen as enumerative. It is *the real people* who have expressed their will
2. *The will of the people* is usually embodied in a leadership elite or individual
3. Minorities and dissenters are not *the real people* and must be enemies or even traitors so there is no pluralism

---

[19] Pitkin (2004, 231). For the notion of 'filter bubble' see e.g., https://en.wikipedia.org/wiki/Filter_bubble and for recent changes and trends in media consumption, including observations concerning filter bubbles and echo chambers, see Newman et al. (2017).

[20] Müller (2017) lists 'seven theses on Populism' in his Conclusion; there are overlaps but our list is rather different.

4. There is, therefore, no role for a political opposition: opposition to *the will of the people* is treachery

5. There is no role for second parliamentary chambers or the like which might limit the execution of *the will of the people*

6. There is no role for institutions such as the courts, or the press, that, traitorously, moderate *the will of the people*.

7. There is no role for elites outside of the leadership which is said to be not an elite itself as it encapsulates *the will of the people*: other elites challenge the leadership and can only be traitors.

8. As we argue in this book, there is no role for bodies of scientific experts, who might moderate *the will of the people*; the government and their entourage encapsulates all the expertise and competing experts can only be traitors.

9. *Crucially*: Populist leaders proclaim all the above without shame; to hide these violations of pluralist democracy would be to reinforce the values that undergird pluralist democracy—to proclaim and embrace these violations is to support *populism* and attack the basic values of democracy.

References

Arditi, B. 2003. Populism, or Politics at the Edges of Democracy. *Contemporary Politics* 9 (1): 17–31.

Collins, Harry M., Sam Finn, and Patrick Sutton. 2001. What Is TWAP? Three Notes on the American Election in the Year 2000. *Social Studies of Science* 31 (3): 428–436.

Douthat, Ross. 2018. The Pull of Populism. *The New York Times*, February 14. https://www.nytimes.com/2018/02/14/opinion/trump-populism-republi-can-party.html

Freedland, Jonathan. 2018. Brexit Reveals Our Political System Is Failing. The 48% Must Have a Voice. *The Guardian*, February 9, UK edition, sec. Opinion. https://www.theguardian.com/commentisfree/2018/feb/09/brexit-political-system-failing-48-per-cent-theresa-may-corbyn-betrayed

Jacobson, Howard. 2017. The Next Time Jacob Rees-Mogg Is Given Screen Time, I Will Break the Television. *The Guardian*, October 21. https://www.theguardian.com/books/2017/oct/21/jacob-rees-mogg-given-screen-time

Judis, John B. 2016. *The Populist Explosion: How the Great Recession Transformed American and European Politics*. New York: Columbia Global Reports.

Keane, John. 2018. Post-Truth Politics and Why the Antidote Isn't Simply 'Fact-checking' and Truth. *The Conversation*, March 23. https://theconversation.com/

post-truth-politics-and-why-the-antidote-isnt-simply-fact-checking-and-truth-87364

Laclau, Ernesto. 2005. *On Populist Reason.* London: Verso.

Leonard, David, and Stuart A. Thompson. 2017. Trump's Lies. *The New York Times,* December 14. https://www.nytimes.com/interactive/2017/06/23/opinion/trumps-lies.html?action=click&contentCollection=Politics&module=RelatedCoverage&region=EndOfArticle&pgtype=article

Levitsky, Steven, and Daniel Ziblatt. 2018. *How Democracies Die.* 1st ed. New York: Crown.

Mouffe, Chantal. 2000. *The Democratic Paradox.* London: Verso.

———. 2018. *For a Left Populism.* London: Verso.

Mudde, Cas. 2017. The Problem with Populism. *The Guardian,* February 27. https://www.theguardian.com/commentisfree/2015/feb/17/problem-populism-syriza-podemos-dark-side-europe

———. 2018. How Can Liberals Defeat Populism. *The Guardian,* February 13. https://www.theguardian.com/commentisfree/2018/feb/13/liberals-populism-world-forum-democracy-5-ideas

Mudde, Cas, and Cristobal Rovira Kaltwasser. 2017. *Populism: A Very Short Introduction.* New York: Oxford University Press.

Müller, Jan-Werner. 2017. *What Is Populism?* London: Penguin Books.

Newman, N., Fletcher, R., Kalogeropoulos, A., Levy, D., and Kleis Nielsen, R. 2017. Reuters Digital News Report 2017. Oxford: Reuters Institute for the Study of Journalism. Retrieved from http://www.digitalnewsreport.org/.

Pitkin, Hanna Fenichel. 2004. Representation and Democracy: A Uneasy Alliance. In *Politics, Judgment, Action,* ed. Dean Mathiowetz, 225–232. Milton Park: Routledge.

Roth, Kenneth. 2017. The Dangerous Rise of Populism: Global Attacks on Human Rights Values. In *World Report 2017,* ed. Human Rights Watch. https://www.hrw.org/sites/default/files/world_report_download/wr2017-web.pdf

Sparrow, Jeff. 2018. *Trigger Warnings: Political Correctness and the Rise of the Right.* Brunswick, VIC: SCRIBE.

Temelkuran, Ece. 2019. *How to Lose a Country: The 7 Steps from Democracy to Dictatorship.* London: 4th Estate.

Urbinati, Nadia. 2006a. *Representative Democracy: Principles and Genealogy.* Chicago: University of Chicago Press.

———. 2006b. Political Representation as a Democratic Process. Edited by K Palonen. *Redescriptions—Yearbook of Political Thought and Conceptual History* 10 (1): 18–40.

Weale, Albert. 2018. *The Will of the People: A Modern Myth.* Cambridge: Polity Press.

World Forum for Democracy. 2017. *Is Populism a Problem?* https://rm.coe.int/world-forum-for-democracy-2017-final-report/16807840c7

CHAPTER 5

What Is Science?

Abstract Since the early 1970s, in social studies of science and technology (STS), the 'logic of scientific discovery' has been displaced by detailed examinations of science in practice; this has eroded the cultural position of scientific expertise. Furthermore, the 'crown jewels' of science, Newtonian physics and the like, are no longer accepted as justifying science's contribution to citizens' more diffuse technical concerns. Scientific expertise now seems more fallible, less removed from ordinary decision-making and less insulated from political and social forces. Populist leaders, who attack scientific expertise because it limits their power, can draw on these ideas. STS must stop celebrating the erosion of scientific expertise and, without sacrificing the new insights, rethink the justification for the role of science in democratic societies.

Keywords Social studies of science and technology (STS) • Erosion of science's role in democracy • Scientific values • Rethinking science's role

CARTOONS AND PRACTICES

We claim in the Introduction that science was understood only in 'cartoon' form before the 1970s 'watershed'. What we mean is that analysts of science tended to try to work out how science *must* work rather than examine how it did work. In so far as analysts examined science in practice

© The Author(s) 2020   47
H. Collins et al., *Experts and the Will of the People*,
https://doi.org/10.1007/978-3-030-26983-8_5

they tended to think that scientists' sketches of their own procedures provided all the information they needed.[1] But as scientists' hero, Richard Feynman, said (or was said to have said), 'The philosophy of science is as useful to scientists as ornithology is to birds'. The usually overlooked corollary is that scientists do not *necessarily* understand science any better than birds understand ornithology; birds can fly without understanding what flying is and scientists can do science without understanding what science is. This is not to say that pre-watershed philosophy, history and sociology of science was not extremely technically accomplished, and even brilliant, simply that it lacked empirical detail.[2] Philosophers would come up with some logical scheme such as Popper's 'falsificationism' and scientists, noting that they did often try to find ways to falsify their claims, would agree that the 'secret of science' was trying to falsify; that is what is meant by a cartoon model of science. Likewise, the sociologist Robert Merton's 'norms of science', insightful though they were, were cartoon-like in so far as they were not based on detailed, technically-based, observations of the day-to-day practices of scientists at work, whether doing routine science or resolving scientific disputes.[3]

The trigger for the sudden expansion of detailed observations of science was probably the philosophical and historical work of ex-physicist, Thomas Kuhn. Kuhn invented the term 'paradigm revolution'. What he meant was that when some rare, major shift, in scientific thinking took place it amounted to a conceptual revolution. He said that what came before and what came after were 'incommensurable'—that is, the new couldn't be measured or assessed on the old scale. For instance, in the Newtonian paradigm, energy was conserved and so was matter, but under the Einsteinian paradigm one could be converted into the other. This meant that the switch from one paradigm to another was not a smooth cumulative process but involved the acquisition of a new set of conceptual 'spectacles' for viewing the world. Kuhn illustrated the point with colourful metaphors such as the 'gestalt switch' that takes place when you see a 'Necker Cube' first one way then another, or the famous drawing that

---

[1] These writings tend to be philosophical or historical in nature, with the work of the Vienna School being a typical example of the approach along with Karl Popper's *Logic of Scientific Discovery* (Popper 2002).

[2] Ludwik Fleck's work on the 'genesis and development of a scientific fact', first published in German in 1935, is a notable exception in its naturalist treatment of scientific practice. See Fleck (2008).

[3] Merton's 'norms of science' can be found in his *Sociology of Science* (Merton 1973).

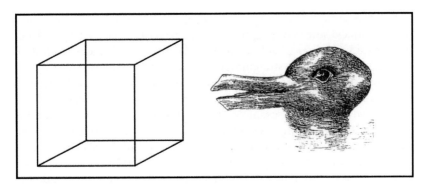

Fig. 5.1 Gestalt switch images analogous to paradigm shifts

sometimes looks like a duck and sometimes like a rabbit depending on which way you look at it (Fig. 5.1). If Kuhn was right the role of science in the world of knowledge must change, for scientific findings were no longer a fixed point against which our perceptions could be verified. As Kuhn put it, we live in different world on the far side of a paradigm shift and if the world was different it was no longer the ultimate judge of what was true and what was not—suddenly it began to look more like fashion or art and the truth of the matter, as Kuhn's critics put it, would be decided by 'mob psychology'.

Inspired by this licence to think differently about science, which was itself just an element in the extraordinary conceptual loosening up in every sphere known as 'the '60s', social analysts began to examine the day-to-day practice of science in more detail. Historians and philosophers were already discovering the cracks in the old picture but the approach was given its major impetus by sociologists and then anthropologists.[4] Some of the ideas were anticipated or even driven by those very few scientists who did know how to reflect upon their own professional lives with sufficient skill to begin to understand the equivalent of Feynman's scorned 'ornithology'; they included Ludwik Fleck, Thomas Kuhn, Peter Medawar, Gerald Holton, and others.[5]

To jump to the present, the detailed observation of scientific practice—treating it as day-to-day work rather than a set of hidden, priestly rituals—

[4] Pioneering studies included Bloor (1973, 1991), Collins (1974, 1975, 1985/1992), Latour and Woolgar (1979), Knorr-Cetina (1981).
[5] See for example: Fleck (2008), Kuhn (1962), Medawar (1967), and Holton (1978).

resulted in some 'debunking' of the mystery of science.[6] Analysts noted that scientific disputes were extremely hard to settle—scientist Max Planck having said (or being said to have said) 'science advances funeral by funeral'—and that the straightforward mechanisms put in place by the philosophers and thought to work by scientists, such as replication of results or falsification of alternatives, did not work or, at least, did not work as advertised. For example, when a scientist failed to replicate the work of another the original scientist would often complain that the replicator had not done the work properly. Because skilful experiment is based on tacit knowledge it is not possible to find an 'objective' criterion for experimental skill so, if heavily disputed, claims about replication and non-replication turn into arguments about the competence of the scientists involved and these will resemble judgements of competing views in non-scientific areas of life; deciding whether an experiment has been replicated can turn out to be not so different to deciding whether this fashion is better than that fashion or this religion is better than that religion.[7] To repeat, this kind of thing detaches science from the determining force of the natural world, at least as far as the short term is concerned. It allows us to see the way that the social and political environment could influence scientific conclusions and numerous case studies have shown the way that it does actually happen.[8]

Scientific 'facts' under this model are not simply the stubborn interventions of nature that they had been thought to be. By changing or questioning the assumptions upon which observations or experiments are based, or by questioning statistical procedures, or by opening up the ground for disagreement about what is 'signal' and what is 'noise', it becomes possible to interpret 'facts' in many ways. These studies showed that scientific claims were subject to great 'interpretative flexibility'—like any other cultural product.

We know from the detailed examination of science that followed this 1970s revolution that the ideal norms of science are not universally followed but we need to be careful about what it is that is being proposed. In all professions, as in any social group, we find a distinction between what, in Chap. 2, we called 'formative aspirations'—the norms that define a

---

[6] For an attempt to make this accessible to a wide audience, see *The Golem* series: Collins and Pinch (1979, 2005, 2010).

[7] This is known as the experimenters' regress Collins (1985/1992).

[8] For early cases see for example: MacKenzie (1981) and Shapin (1979, 2007).

group as a distinctive way of being in the world—and the actual practices, which will often vary from the ideal. Uncovering or understanding the formative aspirations of a group is a matter of sociology. Thus, Popper's *logic* of scientific discovery was *not* an attempt to discover the formative aspirations of science though we would now say that falsification is one of them. Popper's formula was never going to work because social groups do not work according to formulae; falsifiability is an aspiration for science but if a scientist is not engaged in falsification it does not mean they are not doing science. On the other hand, if a social group does not engage from time to time in attempts to specify the conditions under which one or other of its claims could be falsified then it is not a group of scientists; exactly the same goes for the aspiration to corroborate scientific findings, which shows how different the approach is to Popper's. Scientific groups are distinguished by a set of norms and values like this, including honesty, integrity and disinterestedness, aspiration to which define them as scientists irrespective of the countless violations that are encountered in their everyday life. For example, irrespective of occasions of cheating and fraud in science it is easy to distinguish it from, say, business practice. In the latter the defining norm is profit; even though in some businesses the pursuit of profit may be best achieved by generating a reputation for honesty and integrity, the honesty and integrity is instrumental not defining of the activity. In science, however, honesty and integrity are integral to the activity; if you lie about your results you are simply not doing science whereas if you lie about your balance sheet you may well be doing good business. That the values of science can be said to overlap with the values of democracy turns on distinguishing aspiration from actual behaviour.

During the 1980s and '90s the 1970s kind of analysis found itself in competition with an approach that was especially popular among scholars from the humanities. The establishment of scientific facts is a matter of publishing papers in scientific journals and the newer scholars could look at science as a literary endeavour, analysing the life of 'inscriptions' and the way they were modified as a claim moved from an initial observation to a confirmed finding.[9] Science, under this way of thinking, was a matter of creating a carapace of words and the key to understanding it was not philosophy, or even sociology and history, but semiotics. There was no need

---

[9] The most influential, if not the first exponent, of this semiotic style of analysis is Bruno Latour, whose early work laid the foundation for what subsequently became known as Actor-Network Theory. See for example: Latour (1993, 2003), Callon (1986), and Mol (2003).

to understand any of the technical details of the science to understand the way scientific texts created what came to count as the physical world. The tension between the two new approaches continues, united by a discontent with the old 'logic' of scientific discovery but divided about approach, methodology and the substance of scientific knowledge—the social versus the literary.

Tension or not, the general drift is that analysts were finding ways of looking at the creation of scientific knowledge that made science look like any other cultural enterprise such as creation of art or fashion, fields in which what counted as good work was a matter of assembling opinions. Judgements could no longer be guaranteed to be the same across conflicting cultures, local or international, because they were not rigidly constrained by an external reality. Scientific knowledge could be 'constructed' one way 'here' and another way 'there'. To repeat, the way knowledge was constructed could no longer be seen as independent of social and political forces. Detailed case studies showed, to give just two examples, one early, one later, the way statistical procedures, such as the idea of correlation, had been historically influenced by eugenic ideas and how reproductive science was affected by prejudices in respect of women.[10]

Whether one agrees with all this or not, the fact remains that the work associated with all these trends led to a far richer understanding of science: cartoons were replaced by something that better represented science as it was done. We now know that science is much, much harder than the simple models imply and we know that it is impossible to divorce science and scientific findings cleanly from their social environment. We live in a far more interesting but far more complex world when it comes to understanding and defending science, *if defending it is what we want to do*.[11]

---

[10] See MacKenzie (1981), Oudshoorn (1994), and Martin (1991).

[11] Incidentally, this new kind of work on the analysis of science was done under different disciplinary labels. The, Marxist inspired 'social responsibility in science' was a forerunner which took the interrelationship between science, capitalism and socialism as topic. 'Sociology of scientific knowledge' (SSK), grew out of theories based in philosophy and sociology and was dominant through the 1970s and early '80s while more generic terms that were around at the same time were 'science studies' and 'social studies of science'. Today's most widespread label is 'science and technology studies' (STS), though that tends to connote a greater concern with immediate policy issues than with the nature of knowledge.

EMBRACE OF RETHINK?

The 1970s change in the analysis of science could itself be described as a 'paradigm shift' and, in some respects, the term 'mob psychology' would not do violence to the way it was received and assessed. The least edifying reaction was what was known as the 'Science Wars', which comprised scornful attacks by certain scientists and philosophers on the new analysts and their work. They insisted that because scientific knowledge was self-evidently superior, and the consequences of a levelling down of its legitimacy were too awful to contemplate, the analysis must be not only wrong but stupid. Some of the new work was, indeed, careless, driven primarily by iconoclastic passion, but much of it was careful and detailed; in respect of this face of the 1970s revolution, the 'science warriors' were, essentially, abandoning a scientific approach to safeguard science as they wanted it to be.[12] It would have been much better from the beginning if both advocates and detractors had worked together to try to make the findings of the new work compatible with the wide agreement that a good society needed respect for science. As it was, the Science Wars gave rise to polarisation, with each side digging in to defensive positions. It would be a decade or more before it became possible to try to 'square the circle' and then resistance to the new peace proposals came as much from one entrenched side as the other.

What can be seen in retrospect, is that the findings of the new analysts of science can be handled in two ways, even by those who accept them as a sound description: the consequences—a science more intimately related to politics and other social forces—can be embraced and glorified or it can

---

[12] A 'science war' differs from a scientific controversy in so far as the arguers are mostly concerned to convince an outside audience rather than to convince their immediate scientific opponents. In a science war there can be more carelessness about accusations than there would be in proper scientific debate because one is trying to characterise the opponents as holding undesirable positions so as to convince outsiders, whereas to have any hope of convincing scientific opponents one must begin with a full understanding and careful description of their actual views. Some of the more well-known interventions by the critics of this new social understanding of science include: Sokal and Bricmont (1999), Koertge (2000), Gross et al. (1997), and Gross and Levitt (1998). Volume 29 (issue 2) of the journal *Social Studies of Science* contains a number of replies and responses to articles first published in Koertge's (2000) edited collection *A House Built on Sand*. For an exception to these poor quality exchanges, see Labinger and Collins (2001). For an example of belated collaboration evolving out of initial confrontations, see Franklin and Collins (2016). For a more recent discussion of the issue of anti-science, see Durant (2017).

be resisted with the value and the values of science continuing to be endorsed but in more subtle ways. A contributor to the choice of position was probably the tension between 'The Two Cultures'. C. P. Snow's essay by that name, presented in 1959, described the way the sciences, on the one hand, and the arts and humanities, on the other, rivalled each other in intellectual life, driven by social-class-related snobbery. Notably, it was perfectly respectable for someone from the non-science side to flaunt ignorance in public about scientific matters whereas ignorance of artistic or humanistic matters showed a lack of refinement. At the same time, of course, the sciences were lauded for their successes both in the Second World War and its aftermath, with the excitement over nuclear power and the like in full spate. Many of those who engaged in the new analysis of science from the humanities side would naturally find relief in the fact that the sciences were no longer to be seen as giving rise to a kind of knowledge that was unquestionably superior in terms of its truth to their more refined knowledge. Such entrants to the new game would enthusiastically embrace the erosion of the status of the sciences. Many of those entering the new field from a more scientific background would find the new kind of analysis exciting and interesting but would be less likely to celebrate the levelling down of the cultures. For example, one book that became a focus in the Science Wars—Collins and Pinch's, *The Golem*, published in 1993— included the sentiment: 'Let us admire them [scientists] as craftspersons: the foremost experts in the ways of the natural world.'[13] For analysts who shared this kind of sentiment the potentially damaging implications of this post-watershed work were obvious and many felt uneasy after the initial delight in rearranging the order of authority in academic society. But, as intimated, given the entrenched positions of the two sides, it was hard to work out ways to re-establish the value of science under the new analysis.

The other source of the heartfelt embrace of the erosion of science's power and its consequences was the claim that science, because of its esoteric nature, was outside democratic scrutiny; under the new model, even science's findings could be brought back under scrutiny by the people. Given the scope for flexibility in the interpretation of results, and therefore the flexibility about what could be claimed to be true, there was ample scope for scientific outcomes to be affected by social, political and financial forces. Much valuable work was done showing how political influence affected scientific claims. A series of case-studies shows that without doubt

---

[13] Collins and Pinch (1979, 142); this sentiment was ignored by zealots on all sides.

science was biased against the experience-based understanding of working people or that other hidden values were at play when scientists 'framed' the scope of scientific inquiries in a narrow, technical, way. Unfortunately, this kind of sentiment got out of hand and a situation arose where, among certain academically powerful groups, lay-peoples' understanding was described as just as valid as that of technically experienced researchers. Certain social analysts even defended the rights of ordinary peoples' interpretations of vaccine data against those of specialists. The distinction between experts and non-experts was threatened, something that, as we explain in this book, plays into the hands of populist leaders. The popularity of the idea of 'lay expertise' was what finally gave rise to the publication of an explicit attempt to resist the erosion of science in a 2002 paper by two of the current authors. This was vilified by important actors from what we call the 'embrace' persuasion—those who strongly favoured the erosion of science's social and political status—but it has been one of the most widely cited papers in the field of Social Studies of Science, or Science and Technology Studies (STS).[14]

The recent change in political climate has posed a problem for philosophers who believe that a consequence of science's new cognitive status is that scientific values should align better with society's values rather than being proudly independent. For many decades this might have seemed a reasonable stance but seems less attractive now that society's values seem increasingly malign. In such situations we need an independent science to stand up against societies anti-pluralist values, just as we did at the time of 1930s fascism.[15]

STS, unsurprisingly, has found itself having to react to the claim that its erosion of the status of science plays into the hands of post-truth and populism in general. But the response seems half-hearted given the danger of the times. Some STS advocates have preferred to pretend that that the fear of the consequences that could follow from the neo-Kuhnian interpretation of science that drove the science warriors and so many others was misplaced. STS, they say, shows how hard it is to make knowledge, not that knowledge is anybody's. But this seems to falsify the history of the new approach to the social study of science which eroded science's

---

[14] Collins and Evans (2002).
[15] For the most influential version of the philosophical view, see Douglas (2009). Douglas is surely not in favour of populism but she seems not to have considered the implications of her 'responsiveness to society' argument for malign societies.

claims to be an unassailable source of truth. Other supporters of the embrace persuasion take comfort in STS's impotence: 'we are not powerful enough to have had any serious effect on anyone'. But that, even if it is true, is hardly a source of comfort—like saying 'I may express racist sentiments but no one listens so I'm not a racist really'. But, in any case, STS probably has been influential in spite of the declarations of impotence: the thinking behind the lobbies that pay for fake science so as to create uncertainty about the safety of tobacco and global warming understand the 'post-modern' attack on science and know from STS that it is almost impossible to expunge scientific doubts—the studies associated with the sociology of scientific knowledge having provided the detailed explanation why. STS has to grasp the nettle of its influence whether actual or potential, and work out a way to handle it.[16]

The resistance to the erosion of science, the beginning of which is described by Collins and Evans in their 2002 paper as the 'Third Wave of Science Studies', has led on to attempts to rethink ways to handle the problem. So far there have been three interrelated suggestions: first a switch from concentration on the construction of truth—something that we now know we cannot pin down except in the very long term—to concentration on expertise, which can be identified in real time; second, a focus on *the values* of science which remain constant and valuable to democratic societies—even if the science turns out to be wrong in the long term; and third, as we explain in this book, understanding that science is a provider of one of the vital checks and balances in pluralistic democracies.[17] Maybe there are other way to justify the importance of science to democratic societies still to be thought up, but these three, taken together, show us how we can resist the erosion of the cultural and political importance of scientific expertise. To repeat, the choice for those who accept the account of science associate with the 1970s revolution in social studies of science, is whether to embrace the erosion of the cultural authority of science or rethink the justification for the special place of scientific expertise in contemporary society—*embrace* or *rethink*.

---

[16] See, for example, Sismondo (2017a, b), Collins et al. (2017), and Jasanoff and Simmet (2017). Fuller (2016), in contrast to both sides, applauds STS for being in the vanguard of post-truth!

[17] For the first suggestion see Collins and Evans (2002) and Durant (2016); for the second, see Collins and Evans (2017a).

CROWN JEWELS AND ROUGH DIAMONDS

Another of the changes associated with the watershed, but with its roots in something other than close examination of day-to-day scientific practice, was the realisation that there was more to science than its iconic successes. In the heyday of the philosophy of science the problem was taken to be to explain science's major successes such as Newtonian physics, Einstein's revolution, the success of quantum theory and so on—sciences 'crown jewels'. But these accomplishments are very infrequent in comparison to what science does most of the time. Science is applied to all kinds of more difficult problems in the hope that somehow the success exhibited in the crown-jewel accomplishments will licence the authority in the 'rough diamond' areas but, in so far as it does, it is hard to show it. The rough-diamond sciences, and they are by far the more typical of science in terms of the distribution of scientific effort, include long-term weather forecasting, econometric modelling of economies—both notable for their lack of success—and medical, environmental and engineering sciences where scientific judgements are intricately related to social judgments about the priorities, preferences and behaviour of patients or users.[18] Obviously, other things being equal, science has far less independent authority when it belongs to one of these rough-diamond categories and it is tempting to consider that it adds nothing to decision-making processes over and above politics. It is all too easy to extend that kind of judgement to sciences of all kinds. There certainly are many occasions when science and politics have to work closely together to produce a scientific outcome but the two, as we argue here, must remain distinguishable.[19]

[18] The extreme version of this situation, in which the uncertainty and/or the risks of making a mistake are very high has been called post-normal science (Funtowicz and Ravetz 1993) to emphasise the ways the mechanisms that normally ensure quality in scientific work break down. Jasanoff (1990) uses the term 'regulatory science' which describes a distinct domain of scientific knowledge production that is situated at the intersection of science and politics. Salter's (1988) 'mandated science' generally describes science that is used for the purposes of making policy. Crucially, these terms refer to a kind or type of science that is necessarily and inevitably political given that scientific outcomes—say a scientific judgement about the safety of a chemical compound—are intrinsically dependent on social values and political judgements. Without defining what 'safe' means and who has to be kept 'safe' (and who is ignored), no 'scientific' judgement of safety is possible. Examples of science where social judgements are particularly acute/visible include: Bijker (2007), Epstein (1996), Wynne (1992), Hilgartner (2000), Irwin (1995).

[19] An analogy is that mixing science and politics is like mixing oil and water in a bottle: if the bottle is shaken hard, the oil and water are hard to distinguish, nevertheless, the oil stays oil and the water stays water (Collins et al. 2010).

Two Dimensions of the Critique of Science

We could represent the choices available for the assessment of the status of science and its role in decision-making on a graph with an X-axis running from crown-jewels at the origin to the rough diamonds as we move out, and a Y-axis with the full social constructivist or, even, post-modern analysis at the origin, moving out to an old-fashioned 'logic of scientific discovery' interpretation. Table 5.1 is a version of such a graph drawn, for simplicity's sake, not with continuous axes but as a two-by-two table with four extreme possibilities numbered 1–4.

What we want to establish is that even if you endorse the view of science found in box 4—namely that the science you are interested in is rough-diamond science and ineffectual and/or bound up with politics and, in any case, you believe that there is nothing special about science because even crown-jewel science is socially constructed—one should still endorse the authority of science where it is the nature of the natural and social world that is at stake if one wants to preserve democracy as we know and value it. The strategy is that of the 'hard case': if we can establish this for even those who believe that science is found in box 4, then it has to hold for any view of science that is less far along the axes. As argued throughout, this means rethinking the justification we use to support scientific expertise instead of celebrating and embracing the erosion of science's authority.

The old models of science, based on the crown jewels, gave rise to the idea that when science was right it was completely right but when it was not right it was worth nothing—after all, what is the use of an incorrect theory of the movement of the planets or a false theory of relativity. A corollary of this binary view of science is that the notion of *scientific expertise* is intrinsically linked to being right and this fits with most psychological and philosophical models of any kind of expert: an expert is a person that is right or in possession of the truth. In contrast, the new model of scientific expertise takes science to be better described by the term 'sys-

Table 5.1 Ways of thinking about science

	Crown jewels	*Rough diamonds*
Logic of scientific discovery	1	2
Social constructivist/post-modern	3	4

tematic inquiry'. Systematic inquiry does not start out with the certainty that a correct conclusion must be reached to make the enterprise worthwhile, it takes it that the point of the exercise is to work toward a better solution if such can be found. The strength of systematic inquiry, as the term is used here, lies not in the correctness of its results but in the integrity of the search for a better solution. In the case of scientific expertise, at worst, the enterprise will be the search for a solution that cannot be found. Nevertheless, in a democracy, when scientific claims are part of the issue, it has to be better to give special weight to the views of those whose profession's central values include disinterestedness, integrity and a commitment to observation and experiment. To repeat, this is not to say that no scientist ever departs from these value commitments but adherence to these values is more likely when the enterprise itself is a search for truth not profit. Fewer and fewer professions seem able to maintain their integrity are in the face of free-market capitalism—for example, note the transformation of banking—but there may be more hope for science because of its constitutive aims.

Should we choose not to choose scientific experts when we want advice about our pressing technical problems we will hasten the transition to a dystopia where technical conclusions are the preserve of the rich, the strong and the celebrated—it is they who will decide, for instance, if the climate is warming and whether certain vaccines cause autism. Book burning is not far behind.

REFERENCES

Bijker, Wiebe E. 2007. Dikes and Dams, Thick with Politics. *Isis* 98 (1): 109–123. https://doi.org/10.1086/512835.

Bloor, David. 1973. Wittgenstein and Mannheim on the Sociology of Mathematics. *Studies in History and Philosophy of Science Part A* 4 (2): 173–191. https://doi.org/10.1016/0039-3681(73)90003-4.

———. 1991. *Knowledge and Social Imagery*. 2nd ed. Chicago: University of Chicago Press.

Callon, Michel. 1986. Some Elements of a Sociology of Translation: Domestication of the Scallops and the Fishermen of St Brieuc Bay. In *Power, Action and Belief: A New Sociology of Knowledge?* ed. John Law, 196–223. London: Routledge. http://ionesco.sciences-po.fr/com/moodledata/3/Callon_Sociology Translation.pdf.

Collins, Harry. 1974. The TEA Set: Tacit Knowledge and Scientific Networks. *Science Studies* 4 (2): 165–185.

————. 1975. The Seven Sexes: A Study in the Sociology of a Phenomenon, or the Replication of Experiments in Physics. *Sociology* 9 (2): 205–224. https:// doi.org/10.1177/003803857500900202.

Collins, Harry. 1985/1992. *Changing Order: Replication and Induction in Scientific Practice.* Chicago: University of Chicago Press. [1992 = second edition]

Collins, Harry M., and Robert Evans. 2002. The Third Wave of Science Studies: Studies of Expertise and Experience. *Social Studies of Science* 32 (2): 235–296. https://doi.org/10.1177/0306312702032002003.

Collins, Harry, and Robert Evans. 2017a. *Why Democracies Need Science.* Cambridge and Malden, MA: Polity Press.

Collins, Harry, Robert Evans, and Martin Weinel. 2017. STS as Science or Politics? *Social Studies of Science* 47 (4): 580–586. https://doi.org/10.1177/ 0306312717710131.

Collins, Harry M., Sam Finn, and Patrick Sutton. 2001. What Is TWAP? Three Notes on the American Election in the Year 2000. *Social Studies of Science* 31 (3): 428–436.

Collins, Harry M., and Trevor J. Pinch. 1979. The Construction of the Paranormal: Nothing Unscientific Is Happening. *The Sociological Review* 27 (1_suppl): 237–270. https://doi.org/10.1111/j.1467-954X.1979.tb00064.x.

————. 2005. *Dr. Golem How to Think about Medicine.* Chicago: University of Chicago Press.

Collins, Harry M, and Trevor Pinch. 2010. *The Golem at Large: What You Should Know about Technology.* 6th Print. Cambridge: Cambridge University Press.

Collins, Harry M., Martin Weinel, and Robert Evans. 2010. The Politics and Policy of the Third Wave: New Technologies and Society. *Critical Policy Studies* 4 (2): 185–201. https://doi.org/10.1080/19460171.2010.490642.

Douglas, Heather E. 2009. *Science, Policy, and the Value-Free Ideal.* Pittsburgh, PA: University of Pittsburgh Press.

Durant, Darrin. 2016. The Undead Linear Model of Expertise. In *Political Legitimacy, Science and Social Authority: Knowledge and Action in Liberal Democracies,* ed. M. Heazle and J. Kane, 17–37. London: Routledge.

————. 2017. Who Are You Calling 'Anti-science'? How Science Serves Social and Political Agendas. *The Conversation,* July 31. https://theconversation. com/who-are-you-calling-anti-science-how-science-serves-social-and-political-agendas-74755. [Reprinted in *The Conversation Yearbook 2017: 50 Standout Articles from Australia's Top Thinkers.* Edited by John Watson. The Conversation Trust; 66–71]

Epstein, Steven. 1996. *Impure Science: AIDS, Activism, and the Politics of Knowledge.* Berkeley: University of California Press.

Fleck, Ludwik. 2008. *Genesis and Development of a Scientific Fact.* Translated by Thaddeus J. Trenn and Fred Bradley. Repr. 11. Aufl (First published in German in 1935). Sociology of Science. Chicago: University of Chicago Press.

Franklin, Allan, and Harry Collins. 2016. Two Kinds of Case Study and a New Agreement. In *The Philosophy of Historical Case Studies, Boston Studies in the Philosophy of Science*, ed. T. Sauer and R. Scholl, 95–121. Dordrecht: Springer.

Fuller, Steve. 2016. Embrace the Inner Fox: Post-Truth as the STS Symmetry Principle Universalized. *Social Epistemology Review and Reply Collective*, December 25.

Funtowicz, Silvio O., and Jerome R. Ravetz. 1993. Science for the Post-Normal Age. *Futures* 25 (7): 739–755. https://doi.org/10.1016/0016-3287(93)90022-L.

Gross, Paul R., and N. Levitt. 1998. *Higher Superstition: The Academic Left and Its Quarrels with Science*. Johns Hopkins Paperbacks ed. Baltimore, MD: Johns Hopkins University Press.

Gross, Paul R., Norman Levitt, and Martin W. Lewis, eds. 1997. *The Flight from Science and Reason*. Baltimore, MD and London: Johns Hopkins University Press.

Hilgartner, Stephen. 2000. *Science on Stage: Expert Advice as Public Drama*, Writing Science. Stanford, CA: Stanford University Press.

Holton, G. 1978. *The Scientific Imagination*. Cambridge: Cambridge University Press.

Irwin, Alan. 1995. *Citizen Science: A Study of People, Expertise, and Sustainable Development*, Environment and Society. London and New York: Routledge.

Jasanoff, Sheila. 1990. *The Fifth Branch: Science Advisers as Policy-Makers*. Cambridge, MA: Harvard University Press.

Jasanoff, Sheila, and Hilton R. Simmet. 2017. No Funeral Bells: Public Reason in a "Post-Truth" Age. *Social Studies of Science* 47 (5): 751–770. https://doi.org/10.1177/0306312717731936.

Knorr-Cetina, Karin. 1981. *The Manufacture of Knowledge*. Oxford: Pergamon Press.

Koertge, Noretta, ed. 2000. *A House Built on Sand: Exposing Postmodernist Myths about Science*. New York: Oxford University Press.

Kuhn, Thomas S. 1962. *The Structure of Scientific Revolutions*. Chicago: University of Chicago Press.

Latour, Bruno. 1993. *We Have Never Been Modern*. Cambridge, MA: Harvard University Press.

———. 2003. *Science in Action: How to Follow Scientists and Engineers through Society*. 11th Print. Cambridge, MA: Harvard University Press.

Latour, Bruno, and Steve Woolgar. 1979. *Laboratory Life: The Social Construction of Scientific Facts*, Sage Library of Social Research, vol. 80. Beverly Hills: Sage Publications.

MacKenzie, Donald A. 1981. *Statistics in Britain, 1865–1930*. Edinburgh: Edinburgh University Press.

Martin, Emily. 1991. The Egg and the Sperm: How Science Has Constructed a Romance Based on Stereotypical Male-Female Roles. *Signs* 16 (3): 485–501.

Medawar, Peter. 1967. *The Art of the Soluble*. London: Methuen.

Merton, Robert King. 1973. *The Sociology of Science: Theoretical and Empirical Investigations*. Chicago: University of Chicago Press.

Mol, Annemarie. 2003. *The Body Multiple: Ontology in Medical Practice*. Durham, NC: Duke University Press.

Oudshoorn, Nelly. 1994. *Beyond the Natural Body: An Archeology of Sex Hormones*. London: Routledge.

Popper, Karl R. 2002. *The Logic of Scientific Discovery*. London and New York: Routledge.

Salter, Liora. 1988. *Mandated Science: Science and Scientists in the Making of Standards*. Dordrecht: Kluwer.

Shapin, Steven. 1979. The Politics of Observation: Cerebral Anatomy and Social Interests in the Edinburgh Phrenology Disputes. *The Sociological Review* 27 (May): 139–178. https://doi.org/10.1111/j.1467-954X.1979.tb00061.x.

———. 2007. *A Social History of Truth: Civility and Science in Seventeenth-Century England*. 4th Print. Science and Its Conceptual Foundations. Chicago: University of Chicago Press.

Sismondo, Sergio. 2017a. Post-Truth? *Social Studies of Science* 47 (1): 3–6. https://doi.org/10.1177/0306312717692076.

———. 2017b. Casting a Wider Net: A Reply to Collins, Evans and Weinel. *Social Studies of Science* 47 (4): 587–592. https://doi.org/10.1177/03063127 17721410.

Sokal, Alan D., and Jean Bricmont. 1999. *Fashionable Nonsense: Postmodern Intellectuals' Abuse of Science*. 1st paperback ed. New York: St. Martin's Press.

Wynne, Brian. 1992. Misunderstood Misunderstanding: Social Identities and Public Uptake of Science. *Public Understanding of Science* 1 (3): 281–304. https://doi.org/10.1088/0963-6625/1/3/004.

How Does Science Fit into Society? The Fractal Model

Abstract According to Studies of Expertise and Experience (SEE), expertise is socialisation into an expert domain. Society consists of many expert domains of different extent, some small and esoteric, some, like language, large and ubiquitous. Expert domains overlap and are embedded within each other like a fractal. Citizens possess 'ubiquitous meta-expertise' which enables them to choose domains when seeking expert opinions—such as whether a vaccine is safe. In such cases, citizens must be ready to treat domains of scientific expertise as more valuable than power or celebrity if we are to avoid dystopia and maintain pluralistic democracy with its checks and balances. Democracies depend on their citizens—'the law of conservation of democracy'; this means we need more civic education to safeguard the future.

Keywords Studies of Expertise and Experience (SEE) • Fractal model • Ubiquitous expertise • Vaccination • The law of conservation of democracy • Civic education

Here we draw together the entire argument of the book. The argument turns on the nature of society, the nature of democracy, the nature of populism and the nature of science. We fill out the 'fractal model', showing what it means to put more democracy into society via civic education and everyday talk and action.

© The Author(s) 2020   63
H. Collins et al., *Experts and the Will of the People*,
https://doi.org/10.1007/978-3-030-26983-8_6

The major new claim of this book is that a certain view of scientific and technical expertise, and the role of science in particular, is *constitutive* of modern democratic societies.[1] We argue, firstly, that this view is central to the culture of such societies and that secondly, scientific and technical experts contribute to the separation of powers and the checks and balances in such societies, fulfilling a similar constitutional role to that of legal institutions and a free press. We have pointed out in the Introduction that the worry that scientific experts are essentially unaccountable to the people is misplaced. We note also that in the case of other kinds of expertise, such as that of judges, it is not thought that the danger of their over-ruling the public should be avoided by replacing their views with the view of the public.

Actually, the law is a 'softer' case since it is agreed in democracies that, in the long term, law and public opinion should reflect each other even if the rule of law is independent in the short term. Furthermore, sheriffs, and certain other legal officials in the USA and perhaps in other countries, are elected, but this is unusual and when it goes too far, such as when partisan politics crudely influences the appointment of supreme court judges, it is usually condemned. Whichever way things are in respect of legal expertise, it remains a frightening prospect for most of us to imagine that scientific expertise should become subject to public opinion even in the long term ways in which it affects the law and, dystopian imaginings aside, we cannot imagine scientists being elected to their posts by the public.

Usually we think it is the government's choice and use of experts, and the generation of policy using expert advice, that has to be accountable to the public. That way the institutions of science and technology are still accountable to the public, but only indirectly. Were the government to fall

---

[1] The overall thrust of this section was prefigured in analyses completed before the dangers of the revival of populism became apparent. In a paper entitled 'The politics and policy of the third wave', Collins, Weinel and Evans argued for 'democracies which actively promote discussion and debate of technical matters yet which reject populism of all kinds', while in the book, *Why democracies need science*, Collins and Evans argued that there is a strong overlap between the values of science and the values of democratic politics so science can lead or reinforce democracies. See Collins et al. (2010, 185) and Collins and Evans (2017b). Ezrahi (1990), offers another version of the symbiosis between science and democracy: scientific rationality enables the administration a democratic state to present itself as a-political. For a thorough survey of theories of the relationship between science and democracy, see Thorpe (2008).

entirely under the thrall of science, we would have a technocracy, and technocracy is to be resisted, but so is the public or political direction of scientific findings.

STUDIES OF EXPERTISE AND EXPERIENCE

Our claim about the cultural role of science grows out of a certain way of looking at the world which starts with what we have said in Chap. 2 about the organic, collective, constitutive element of societies. We combine this with an understanding of expertise and find that that they are two sides of the same coin. This way of looking at the world was developed under a program known as 'Studies of Expertise and Experience' (SEE). It might well be possible to reach the same position from other starting points but SEE is not hard to understand so we will use it to reach the place we want to reach.

The key to SEE is that the larger part of an expertise is 'tacit knowledge'—knowledge or abilities that we possess but cannot explicate and may not even know that we possess.[2] We have already explained that speaking fluent English involves putting the verb in the middle of the sentence but that when we are learning to speak English as a native we have no idea *that* we are putting the verb in the middle of the sentence nor do we know anything much else about how we form good sentences and the like: the language speaking skills of native language speakers are tacit, at least for the first years of their acquisition.[3] The acquisition of fluency in a native language, as well as being an example which is readily accessible to all, has two other special advantages. First it reveals a difference between SEE and most other ways of looking at skills or expertises. Most other models take it that an expertise is essentially something esoteric and hard

---

[2] Michael Polanyi is usually credited with creating the term 'tacit knowledge' (Polanyi 1966). For a more recent analysis of the concept that distinguishes between three different types of tacit knowledge, see Collins (2010).

[3] There is a substantial literature that examines the role of experience and practice in the acquisition of knowledge. The classic examples are riding a bicycle, playing chess driving a car, problems with artificial intelligence and education (H. L. Dreyfus 1979, 1992; Collins 1990; Collins and Kusch 1998; Lave and Wenger 1991). The five-stage model developed by Stuart and Hubert Dreyfus is the most well-known articulation of a stage theory moving from articulated knowledge to unconscious performance (H. L. Dreyfus and Dreyfus 1986; S. E. Dreyfus 2004).

won—for instance, the idea that acquiring a skill takes 10,000 hours.[4] Also, many analyses of expertise take it that an expert is someone who knows better than a non-expert—something that creates problems for the fact that experts often disagree with each other and what counts as even scientific truth changes as time passes and so not every expert can be right. SEE sidesteps these problems by treating the extent to which an expertise is esoteric as a variable: nearly every member of a society develops fluency in the native language at an early age and yet this is a deep and rich expertise, whereas hardly any of them develop an ability in, say, gravitational wave physics. SEE, then, posits a range of expertises from 'ubiquitous' to specialist—a scale of 'esotericity'.[5] Furthermore, SEE makes no assumption about the rightness or necessary efficacy of expert knowledge. While there may be something absolutely right about astronomy, most people would agree that there is nothing absolutely right about astrology; but astrology is just as much an expertise as English-language speaking. If you have not had a training in speaking the language of astrology you will not be able to pass as an astrologer in front of astrologers.[6] Likewise, there is nothing absolutely right about tea-leaf reading or divining a witch using the poison oracle but both are skilful activities, and possession of the relevant accomplishments and 'practice languages'—the ways of speaking associated with being an expert in these fields—would be clear to other

---

[4] Ericsson et al. (1993).

[5] For more on this three-dimensional model of expertise, see Collins (2013).

[6] The idea of being able to 'pass' as a member of a different social group through mastery of their language has been investigated using a new research method developed using concepts from SEE. Known as the Imitation Game, and related to the famous Turing Test, it can be used to explore the extent to which social interactions between groups enable members of one group to take the position of the others by providing answers to questions that are indistinguishable from those provided by members of the target group. Note that this is not a question of 'faking' expertise or pretending to have knowledge as the Imitation Game test can be passed only if the answers provided by the 'Pretender' are seen to be plausible when compared to those provided by someone who is a member of that group. The method can be used across a range of scales and topics, including the extent to which social science fieldworkers understand their participants' worlds (Giles 2006; Collins 2016); how the colour-blind, blind and those with perfect pitch understand the world of the majority culture (Collins and Evans 2014; Collins et al. 2006); the way English and Scottish nationalities compare in cultural recognisability (Evans et al. 2019); and the extent to which males and females understand each other's perspective (Collins and Evans 2014, 2017b). See also Evans and Crocker (2013), Wehrens (2014) and Wehrens and Walters (2017).

experts in these fields.[7] This way of thinking enables us to say that, for example, econometric modelling of economies is an expertise—and an exceptionally esoteric expertise to boot—without having to worry about whether or not it is produces correct results in any absolute sense.[8]

The other great advantage of using fluency in natural language as the paradigm of the acquisition of expertise is that it is acquired via a process of 'socialisation'. SEE takes it that nearly all expertises, being largely comprised of tacit knowledge, are acquired this way. Sometimes the socialisation is referred to as 'apprenticeship' but apprenticeship and socialisation are the same thing; the young child is undergoing an apprenticeship in native language speaking, the novice gravitational wave physicist, or carpenter, or astrologer, undergoes socialisation among experts in order to acquire the specialist expertise, including the language. As intimated, the crucial feature of SEE that takes us where we want to go is that socialisation and the acquisition of expertise are one and the same thing.

GROUPS AND THE FRACTAL MODEL

In the previous paragraph we have quite self-consciously mixed up large and small examples of apprenticeship/socialisation which usually correspond to the ubiquitous-esoteric categorisation. Ubiquitous expertises are large-scale, belonging to every member of a society—things like fluency in the native language and all the other features of a national culture that make the culture what it is; esoteric expertise are small-scale, still belonging to every member of a 'society' but what we are calling the 'societies' of gravitational wave physicists, carpenters and astrologers are small and narrow. Notice also that the tacit knowledge of these groups, big and small, is what constitutes them as groups. The very tacitness and lack of self-consciousness of most of what is learned in the course of socialisation or apprenticeship means that participants in these groups do not *choose* what they take for granted and how they act when they are acting as a member of the group; the way they act and the things they take for granted constitute the group and is part of the way of life of the group just as much

---

[7] The concept of 'interactional expertise' gives rise to the notion of practice languages and allows that such socialisation can be solely through immersion in the spoken discourse of the group. For more on interactional expertise, see Collins (2004, 2011, 2015).

[8] Certain analyses suggest it is usually an unreliable expertise (Evans 1999, 2014).

as putting the verb in the middle of the sentence is part of the way of life of being an English-speaker.[9] The group is not made up of the balance of enumerated decisions, it is constituted by the uniform similarity of action and belief of all, or nearly all, its members, against which background certain discrete, self-conscious choices will be made: this how it is that English speakers are what they are; this is how it is that gravitational wave physicists are what they are; this is how it is that carpenters are what they are; this is how it is that astronomers are what they are; and this is how it is that astrologers are what they are.

Not all classes of person are social groups in this way: there are what one might call 'demographic classifications' as opposed to social groups.[10] Thus, one can identify a group of people whose shoes are brown, and another group whose shoes are black, but wearing a certain colour of shoes is not an expertise and nor does it comprise a social group—you don't need an apprenticeship or socialisation to wear black shoes nor to wear brown shoes.[11]

All these qualities and features, then, apply to all such expert/social groups from big to small: they are constituted out of the actions and beliefs of their members, namely, nearly all of what their members know and believe they know and believe tacitly; unless they are unusually reflective, they will not even know what they know and believe. These same features apply from the largest scale to the smallest scale so the mathematical notion of the 'fractal', where the geometry and features of the top level are preserved when smaller and smaller scale versions of it are reproduced and embedded within one another, is a rough fit to what we are talking about. An example of a fractal structure is a cauliflower: there are florets, within florets, within florets, exhibiting the same geometry at every scale. We are saying that the same thing applies to the cascade of social groups that come into focus in turn as the scale diminishes. We are dealing with an analogy here not an exact mathematical model, and it will not work

---

[9] Incidentally, as we will mention again in the main text, seen from inside the group, these specialist, taken-for-granted, ways of going on are part of the ubiquitous expertise *of the specialist group*.

[10] Brubaker (2002) argues for caution when using the label 'social group' and warns of 'groupism'.

[11] But if such a demographic classification, such as those with red or ginger hair, decide to define themselves as a social group, or if wider society is prejudiced against such a group, a simple classification like this can give rise to self-conscious 'groupishness'; there is a small movement of this sort in respect of red or ginger hair; see http://redheaddayuk.co.uk/.

perfectly because the way social groups are embedded within one another is multidimensional and overlapping but the broad picture captures the way the world is.

SEE also discusses meta-expertise, which is the ability to judge between experts whose expertise you do not share. Of particular importance to the argument presented here is citizens' meta-expertise; this is a 'ubiquitous expertise'. As explained, in contrast to most theories, which treat expertise as the hard-won possession of elites, SEE allows for ubiquitous as well as specialist expertises and allows that citizens have a ubiquitous meta-expertise born of their socialisation that gives them a taken-for-granted way of ranking certain kinds of expert—this is crucial as we will see.[12]

This approach to expertise and, indeed, to the related understanding of the nature of sociological analysis as a whole, takes it that there is a reality to certain social groups—to collectivities or forms of life.[13] Indeed, it has been argued that such groups are defined by the 'formative action types' that characterise them—e.g. divining a witch among the Azande versus taking out a mortgage in the UK. So, does this not invite populism?[14] Could there not be such a thing as the, italicised, *will of the people* once we allow that expertise and the associated groups are real, definable and only fully accessible via social immersion—once we allow that the collectivity might be more basic than the individual in respect of certain fundamentals—once we allow that there are genuine members of society and mere pretenders? It seems there has to be the possibility of such a thing if we are to have a sociology based in the sociology of knowledge and we need to ask whether sociology itself conceived in this way is an invitation to populism. The answer is that it is such an invitation, which is why sociology's notion of the 'collective' is so abhorred in societies that make individual freedom an icon—it smacks of communism and fascism and other forms of subversion of the individual to a greater will.

---

[12] Remember, the difference between mere 'demographic' groups and genuine social groups can be understood by asking whether there is something that belongs to the group in question that a non-member would find it hard to imitate in a question and answer test—there is nothing in the case of brown shoe wearers but lots in the case of, say, cricketers. We have put this test into practice in the Imitation Game research mentioned in Fn. 6 in Chap. 6.

[13] For the point as regards sociological analysis in general, see Collins and Kusch (1998) and Collins (2019).

[14] The term 'formative action types' is taken from Collins and Kusch (1998).

The solution draws on something that has already been explained in Chaps. 2 and 3. It depends on separating the preferences of the people into two types: those that express to 'policy choices' and that arise out of 'formative intentions'. Policy choices are enumerative in that they are the kinds of things that are tested at elections and which appear on election manifestos and form the basis of specific policies: How much debt should the government incur? How much should be spent on the health service? Should private schooling be subsidised? The answers to these questions are tested by enumeration of opinions—by counting and balancing votes (we are talking of the ideal model, recognising that, in the real world, power is always in play). Formative choices, on the other hand, are much more to do with the very constitution of society and are not usually brought into the realm of conscious decision-making even at election times: Should we discriminate against certain groups of citizens according to their race? Should we maintain English as our common language? How do we respond to strangers asking for help? Answers to these kinds of question, as we have discussed in Chap. 2, are generally uniform across the entire population and they *do* constitute something that it is reasonable to call the *will of the people*. But this *will* is not made up of the kinds of things that appear on election manifestos since nearly every citizen would make the same choices and, therefore, they are not normally a potential source of advantage to any political party (except those representing extreme minorities who try to change the constitution of society at the ballot box).

The borderline between the two kinds of choice is not absolutely sharp; for example, a different answer to the language question might be given by a proportion of the population of Wales and Welsh politicians might gain an advantage by giving prominence to the Welsh language in manifestos and race-discrimination is always a potential source of votes, but such cases are the exception rather than the rule. What the ovals (Fig. 6.1) in the fractal model of society show is the groups and sub-groups that are defined by the things they are, things that become natural to the new recruit to the group after a period of participatory socialisation, but which they do not actively *choose* beyond the initial choice of becoming a member of the group. Of course, even membership of certain significant groups is not self-consciously chosen—these groups, include the entire society, where socialisation starts at too young an age to be a matter of choice.

The Fractal Model and the Principle of Conservation of Democracy

Figure 6.1 is a schematic and partial representation of the UK (with only small variations it could be any Western democracy), seen as a fractal-like cascade of social groups of decreasing size. Ubiquitous expertise is the pale topmost oval. Each of the ovals below is constituted by certain specialist expertises which are nevertheless seen as ubiquitous from within that oval—for instance, for gravitational wave physicists, the agreement that gravitational waves should initially be treated in the first instance as though they travel at the speed of light is ubiquitous and so is the relationship between the physical world and mathematics, but these are specialist expertises when seen from above—hence the fractal metaphor.

Going back to the topmost oval, in society as a whole the ubiquitous expertise represented is the knowledge that you need to be a member of that society and live within it without making endless mistakes or *faux pas.* You will need to speak the natural language fluently (or your native-born children will), you will need to know how often to wash and dress and

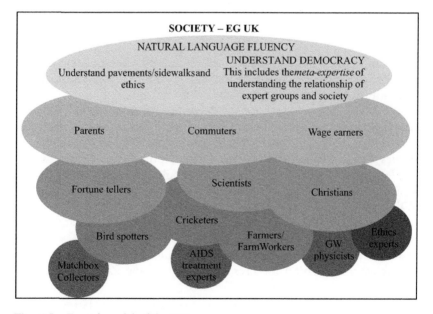

Fig. 6.1 Fractal model of the UK

how close to walk to other people on the pavement (sidewalk) depending on how crowded it is. You will need to have an appropriate sense of ethics and what counts as right and wrong in that society so you don't find yourself inadvertently doing things that will get you locked up and so that the justice system's decisions are widely seen as reasonable and legitimate. We expect nearly every member of, say, UK society to share these expertises and together these kinds of things constitute the society—they are its culture—the organic face. We would not expect such few persons as did not share these expertises to have their own political representatives or be taken into account as contributing to the plural nature of UK society (with, as mentioned, the possible exception of groups such as monoglot Welsh-speakers). To repeat, these kinds of characteristics do constitute the metaphysical character of a society as a social grouping yet, at the same time, they could not form the ideological basis of populism because a party claiming to represent the people, in so far as they believe in not killing or stealing, in putting the verb in the middle of the sentence, walking a reasonable distance from others on the sidewalk, and washing every now and again, though it could be claimed to be representing the will of the people, would not be politically appealing because nearly everyone in the society shares the view so it could not be the foundation of a distinctive political identity (except at times of exceptional political flux). To make political headway populists' claims must be of a kind that have the potential to appeal to a large proportion of the society *and* exclude a sizeable minority of people or ideas, with the aim of turning these exclusions into a constitutive feature of society.

What is to stop any government declaring that it represents *the will of the people* and acting accordingly? According to Levitsky and Ziblatt, the crucial safeguard for democracies are political parties. The role of political parties is to use their selection mechanisms to prevent demagogues standing for political office. They give the examples of Henry Ford, Charles Coughlin, Huey Long, Joseph McCarthy, Charles Lindbergh and George Wallace as political figures with great public followings in America whose careers were stopped by the party machine (Long was assassinated before this could happen).[15] They consider that the American political system has now broken down in this respect, resulting in Trump taking the Republican nomination for President. Levitsky and Ziblatt, along with

---

[15] Levitsky and Ziblatt (2018). McCarthy, of course, generated public hysteria about the threat of communists. For one example of the impact, see Thorpe (2008).

other commentators, also consider that American politics is now so partisan that the Republican party, having reluctantly found itself with Trump at its head, has ceased to take responsibility for its leader or play any further role in the system of checks and balances.[16] The Republican party has, over decades, also violated the unwritten norms that have to be accepted to make the formal mechanisms of the institutions of normal democratic politics work. These norms are 'mutual tolerance'—that means treating the opposition parties with respect even though they disagree with you (in the UK this is enshrined in the phrase 'loyal opposition') and 'institutional forbearance', which means not exploiting every loophole in the written constitution so as to render the ruling party impotent.[17]

Levitsky and Ziblatt do not discuss the more sociological point that is being made with the idea of the law of conservation of democracy, namely that the general population needs to know the nature of democracy if democracy is to flourish. It must be true that the government cannot be held to account by the populace even for actions which are blatantly and unashamedly incompatible with democracy if the populace do not understand what they are witnessing because they do not understand what democracy is! Worse, populists, with their proclamations, are falsely educating a public, already overburdened with a clamour of partisan and extreme views, about what democracy means. Trump's supporters—a frighteningly large proportion of the population of the US at the time of writing (2018/early 2019)—do not seem to understand that he is violating the unwritten rules of their constitution and they, backed by the Republican Party, show no inclination to hold him to account.

Perhaps there has always been a deficit in the understanding of democracy among a substantial proportion of the American population. The more likely alternatives are that a proportion of American citizens once understood democracy and no longer understand it, or that a proportion

---

[16] E.g. Brooks (2017, 2018). Runciman (2018), argues that the pull of personal recognition is eroding political parties. This theme of the decline in political parties is further echoed by Mounk (2018a, b); many indicators point to dissatisfaction with particular political parties turning into distrust in democratic politics itself.

[17] For example, refusing to appoint nominated supreme court judges, filibustering at every opportunity, and many more possibilities of which the Republican party have availed themselves of in recent years. Thomas Frank (2008) describes these dynamics as destroying government so that you can then claim government is too incompetent to trust with the economy meaning that only entrepreneurs and the market can do the job of 'governing'.

of American citizens who understand democracy no longer want it: perhaps their long-standing sense of being neglected under 'elitist' pluralist democracy has led them to think that the only hope is a revolution whose leader is ready to cast democracy aside. Both of the latter possibilities align with the persistence of cultural icons representing the Confederacy in the Civil War, the widespread felt need for guns to be widely available to citizens so they have the potential to defend their communities against 'big government' and its elected representatives, and the long history of electoral near-success of the many non-democrats listed by Levitsky and Ziblatt (note 15). The UK, for example, does not seem to have been beset by these kinds of undemocratic indicators, or at least, not to such a great and regular extent. It is true that the 'will-of-the-people' rhetoric, and the success of populists such as Nigel Farrage, are worrying features of the Brexit debate, but it is hard to generalise from such happenings given that political life in the UK has, for the moment, become so narrowly concentrated on a single issue. Of course, what we have seen in both countries recently is determined politicians trying to change the peoples' understanding of what democracy is, and this is another way to make traditional forms of democracy unaccountable and therefore vulnerable.

Levitsky and Ziblatt and others are dismissive of the ability of the public to limit populist governments in the way we suggest is possible—to repeat, according to their analysis, the long list of demagogues they discuss were stopped by party machines![18] But, surely, as we have suggested, if democratic norms were more widely invested in the American public, figures like Ford, Coughlin, Long, McCarthy, Lindbergh and Wallace, with their explicit anti-democratic rhetoric, would never have gained a following in the first place and, to repeat, such persons do not seem to appear with such regularity in the UK and other countries.[19]

[18] To what extent citizens actually do know understand democratic politics has been empirically investigated and the results are not reassuring (Achen and Bartels 2016, 299). Bartels (1996, 194) claimed that political ignorance amongst US electors is amongst the best-documented of research findings. More recently Friedman (2006) suggested that political ignorance is more widespread than most realize, and Somin's (2013, 17–37) review of the empirical literature led him to conclude that the degree of political ignorance amongst American electors borders on the shocking.

[19] Levitsky writes, in contrast (private communication to Collins, 17 February 2018), '… we emphasize the role of elites, working on the assumption that demagogues will occasionally have appeal in all societies. It's true that we have seen fewer of them in the UK, Canada, and other Western European democracies, at least since 1945. My hunch is that the difference lies in some combination of economic inequality and racial diversity.'

The principle of conservation of democracy also fits with the emphasis put on civic education by the pioneers of democracy and today's leading political analysts.

> From Plato to Cicero, and from Machiavelli to Rousseau, all of them were obsessed with how to instil political virtue in the youth. … What, George Washington asked in his Eighth Annual Address, could be more important than to pass civic values down to the "future guardians of the liberties of this country"?[20]

> In the aftermath of the collapse of Weimar and the rise of Nazism in a highly educated, advanced nation, much of political science in the 1940s–1960s was devoted to asking "Why Weimar?" … The relevant literature is huge … Education in civics was one important sub-strand of that work. But all that literature tended to die out in the late 1960s, [and] By the 1970s it … was dead, alongside civic education itself … in the late 1990s … the question of the preconditions for stable democracy began to attract more attention, a trend that has for obvious reasons sharply accelerated in the last 5–10 years.[21]

Our argument is that we need to put more democracy into society if we are to get democracy out again. This means building the culture which provides citizens with their taken-for-granted understanding of how democratic societies are run. At the moment that cultural understanding, far from being reinforced, is increasingly being eroded by the actions and statements of rulers. How do you change the cultural background against that kind of opposition? For authors such as ourselves the only thing is to do what we have always done—talk about what democracy is in every possible setting. This book is one small contribution to that process; we are trying to create culture here and now. We hope those with more political skills, experience and energy will confront the problem in their way. We believe more formal civic education should also be revived if we are to preserve a lasting pluralist democracy. Education is always a process of socialisation, not just the delivery of information: the very fact that

---

[20] From an essay (Mounk 2018a, b, 57) by Harvard academic and author of *The People vs Democracy: Why Our Freedom is in Danger and How to Save It*. Mounk goes on to say, 'amid an era of unprecedented peace and prosperity, the idea that support for self-government had to be won anew with each passing generation started to fade. Today it is all but extinct.'

[21] Robert Putnam, Malkin Professor of Public Policy at the Kennedy Business School, Harvard University, and author of the 1993, *Making Democracy Work* (private communication to Collins, 10 March 2018).

something is being taught is an expression of its value; the very encouragement of practical activities such as voting or actively participating in civic life is an encouragement to engage in actions that are the counterpart of the concepts being advanced. In our model, this education/socialisation would, among other things, address the role of science in society. Under our conception, the dangers of dishonest application of expertise and the dangers of technocracy would have a vital but subsidiary role in the new civic education with the main emphasis being on explanation of the positive role of scientific experts in democratic society.

Science

As sociologists of science, our preferred description of science would *not* be the dangerous and brittle, 'revelatory' model of the scientist as priest or magician, nor the closely related, 'crown jewels' model which identifies science by reference to its fabulous successes and forgets the rest; these are the models which generally inform the 'public understanding of science', when it is not trying to teach ordinary people more science in the hope that this will generate respect. Science is esoteric, you cannot teach it to everyone, and science is fallible not revelatory, so these efforts tend to amount to advertising or propaganda for science. The preferred model of the authors of this book is the 'craft work with integrity' (CWI) model, which takes the scientist to be an honest craftsperson, doing their best, informed by noble values, but inevitably fallible.[22] The honest admission of fallibility insulates the scientific profession against the inevitable falls from grace of the magician or priest. Fallibility still allows that these people are the least likely to be corrupt and still have the most experience when it comes to exploration of the natural world and that is why they remain the first people to ask if the best technical advice is to be obtained. That said, their word cannot always be the final word because they are fallible and we do not want technocracy, but it should be the undistorted *first* word on how the world actually works (not what to do about it).

---

[22] For more on models of science see Collins (2017, 306ff). As explained an early but overlooked statement of this kind of model is found in a book which became a central target in the science wars—*The Golem* (Collins and Pinch 1979). To repeat, on page 142 Collins and Pinch write: 'Let us admire them [scientists] as craftspersons: the foremost experts in the ways of the natural world'.

Unfortunately, the way science sells itself is mostly quite unsuited to this task because the marketing always falls back on the standard scientific icons: Newton, Einstein, Quantum Theory and so on. Brilliant though these episodes are as exemplary human achievements, along with Collins's favourite, gravitational wave detection, they do not represent the kind of science that the citizen needs to understand—that kind of science has to do with the weather, with diet, with ageing, with vaccination, with economics, and so on—areas of the world which are complex and don't lend themselves to glamorous and convincing solutions. The problem is easy to see with a simple exercise that anyone can try—at least, it works in 2019 and we can only hope it won't work for much longer. Type the word 'science' into Google and then click on 'images'. Then think about how to convince the citizen that scientists have the best understanding of global warming and look through the graphic images that represent science. Which of these would reassure the citizen? Unfortunately, not a single one because they all represent the wrong image of science—rather than painstaking craftwork in the context of a complex reality, we see crown jewels and glossy triumphalism.[23] Science is selling itself in the wrong marketplace if it is to do its most important job—which is to support democracy.

That said, there is hope for a science that can lead and aid democracy if science is allowed to be science—that is an institution defined by the search for the truth about the natural world. There is the constant danger that the pressure on resources will force science to present itself as a source of entertainment or driver of capitalism; it is both of these but neither must become science's *raison d'etre* and that, once more, is a matter of political culture.

SCIENCE AND TECHNOLOGY STUDIES

In this valuation of science as central to good societies, our argument departs from the tendency of contemporary studies of science and technology studies. We believe it is impossible and undesirable to undo the new analyses of science that began in the 1970s but we also believe that the wrong conclusions were widely drawn concerning what that revolution meant. As discussed in Chap. 5, the 'science warriors' feared that the

---

[23] Collins discovered this when preparing a talk using PowerPoint and needing a graphic image to represent science. To find a suitable one he had to search for images relating to 'craftsperson' and to 'committee' because there was nothing suitable under 'science'.

diminution of the authority of science immanent in sociology of scientific knowledge would lead to the kind of political consequences that we see before us:

> The health of liberal democracy depends on the general use of reason. Reason must not be the cognitive tool of the few: if the integrity of science and reason are undermined among the majority, then democracy itself is in peril. (Gross et al. 1997, 491)

The science warriors' understanding of the importance of science in Western democracies was sound but simply equating it with reason was not. What they failed to see was that the problem initially uncovered by the sociology of scientific knowledge was their problem as much as anyone else's and that the solution could not be a simple return to the idea of science prevalent before the 1970s. The choice is whether to embrace, or even celebrate, the intermingling of science and society across the board—the erosion of science—or to strive, despite the inevitable difficulties, to rethink the justification of the special status of science. To resist the erosion it is necessary to strive to maintain the idea of a science whose substantive findings are as free from all political and economic influences as possible even while recognising that science in practice can never be pure. In other words, recognise the intermingling of science and society but resist the transmutation of science into politics or commerce. This choice cannot be sidestepped by anyone who understands democracy and its relationship to populism; we are all contributors to political culture.

In our preferred world, the role of virtuous experts as contributors to the checks and balances—as part of the constitution—would be explained as part of civic education, with the fractal model in the background. Civic education is necessary but will never be sufficient. What is required is something more sociological, namely that the regular practices of democracy be actively executed and spoken of so as to preserve the habits and language that constitute a democratic society's culture; in short the culture of democracy must not only be continually recreated but preserved within a society's taken for granted ways of being in the world. Political parties have a role in this while STS's role is in the way it acts out the relationship between science and society. STS's contribution to civic enculturation must be a shifting of the balance toward understanding that we still need science to support democracy in spite of science's newly revealed fallibility. The way public disputes about the introduction of new technologies, the reaction to vaccine controversies, and so on, are conducted in a society would be a part of the maintenance of its democracy; STS has a lead role in these things and cannot hide under a cloak of impotence.[24]

Ubiquitous Meta-expertise and a New Separation of Powers

We can repeat some of this another way. As already intimated, another constitutive feature of democracies, which is part of citizens' understanding of the nature of pluralist democracy, is included in the ubiquitous meta-expertise of citizens. To live in more or less any kind of society you need 'meta-expertise'. For example, you need what we can call 'sociological meta-expertise' to know how far familiar social expectations extend: thus, you need to know that taxi-drivers pretty well everywhere are likely to be trustworthy or you would never dare get in a cab. Without some meta-understanding of how regular institutions like this extend, to venture beyond your front-door would be a fearsome adventure. The crucial feature of ubiquitous meta-expertise as far as this analysis is concerned, and it has been mentioned once or twice, is an understanding of the relationship between all the other more specialist expertises that are found in the society's 'fractal'. Thus, meta-expertise is what keeps you listening to your school-teachers, going to the dentist, stops you going to the garage instead of the hospital when you break your arm but going to the garage when your car has a problem, and what stops most people in Britain from refusing a blood transfusion when doctors say you need it while certain church leaders say you do not. The constituents of the fractal, and the meta-expertise that gives rise to citizens' understanding of the shape of the fractal, characterise the nature of a society. Notice that this kind of meta-expertise can vary even among pluralist democracies: the relative status of religious and political institutions is very different in the US and the UK.

The new thing we are arguing here is that democracy proper needs a similar, if less formal, separation of powers when it comes to scientific and technological issues. What we mean is that one part of the ubiquitous meta-expertise of citizens has to be the ability to judge the value of the knowledge contributions of groups lower down the fractal in which they do not participate. Within broad limits the population of every democracy proper must share a broadly similar 'civic epistemology' that guides what is

---

[24] This fits well with Levitsky and Ziblat's (e.g. note 13) 'Democracies work best—and survive longer—where constitutions are reinforced by unwritten democratic norms'. Durant (2018, 2019), outlines some of the norms and assumptions that obstruct a view of experts as partners not enemies in a democracy.

expected by way of evidence in public decision-making and identifies who is to be recognised as able to provide that evidence.[25] More specifically, we want to argue that pluralist democracies require that the population is constituted by those with the meta-expertise needed to understand that science is characterised by a set of norms essentially based around honesty and integrity even though, as with any other institution, there will be violations. Citizens must understand that judgements to do with the nature of the world that are based on systematic observation and experiment done in accordance with science's values and norms, even though they may turn out to be wrong, should be treated as better than judgements based on myths, the contents of old books, astrological divination, celebrity, power of all sorts, and the like. It is also better than subjective, emotional, certainty. Note that citizens already understand, as part of what they put into democracy, that judgements concerning criminal guilt are better made by courts of law than by reference to myths, the contents of old books, astrological divination, subjective emotional certainty and the like even though the law sometimes gets it wrong and sometimes lawyers and judges are corrupt. It is no surprise that fascism is often associated with beliefs that allow a level of interpretation that gives their upholders free rein in respect of both science and law and place no constraints on leaders' political choices.

There are a lot of things that this need for a certain kind of meta-expertise does not imply. It does not imply technocracy in the same way the maintenance of a free press does not imply government by the press. In the last resort the output of scientists' procedures and methods cannot determine a policy—policy is made by the political process—technical expertise can only be an input to policy-making. What is necessary if scientific expertise is to act as a check and balance is that it be *explicitly uninfluenced* by politics and its claims be presented in the public forum without distortion.[26] After this it all a matter of accountable politics.[27]

---

[25] Jasanoff (2005) invented the useful term 'civic epistemology'; see Miller (2008) for a general discussion. Here we give the term a more general meaning within which the varying civic epistemologies found in different societies are specific applications within an overall understanding of how knowledge is arranged in pluralist democracies.

[26] This is not a matter of 'making policy'; we do not argue that scientific experts should contemplate, frame and solve policy-relevant problems in academic isolation—framing of policy issues does require input from citizens.

[27] As two of us put it elsewhere, 'Democracy cannot dominate every domain—that would destroy expertise—and expertise cannot dominate every domain—that would destroy democracy' (Collins and Evans 2007, 8). The argument is also made in Collins et al. (2010). For other discussions of the relationship between science and politics, see: Brown (2009), Pielke (2007), Sarewitz (2016).

Under this model, science and technology are less powerful as a constraint on government than the law since it is generally agreed that governments can be absolutely prohibited by the law from certain choices (unless they first engage in a democratic process to change the law); this is not the case with technical advice. Science and technology are more like the press in terms of their power and in the way there can be serious disagreements among scientists, but different in that we would not expect the equivalent of *Fox news* or *Breitbart* or the *National Enquirer* to have any power. In science the equivalent of these is, and has to be, relegated to the status of 'the fringe' that can be safely ignored: a constitutive feature of science is the quest for consensus even though it is brought about through organised scepticism.[28] The aim of argument in science has to be to reach a consensus unaffected by politics and other values even if, for periods of time, such a thing may not be attainable. It has been argued elsewhere that a solution to certain problems is to set up a special committee to determine what counts as scientific consensus at the relevant time and what is the strength of that consensus; the committee would be called 'The Owls'.[29] What makes the Owls different from every other kind of advisor or advisory committee of this type is that it would include social scientists who understand science through the new model of science that began to develop in the 1970s but they would be of a *rethink* persuasion. This way the members of the committee would know how hard it is to work out what the consensus is in the face of contributions from the fringe and other disaffected but scientifically qualified and seriously motivated

----

[28] For the fringe, see Collins et al. (2017). One way in which fringe science is different is that it over-values scepticism and novelty and thus refuses to accept the consensus for far longer than would ordinarily be seen as reasonable.

[29] The committee of the Owls is suggested by Collins and Evans in *Why Democracies Need Science* (2017a). The idea is that, where a policy-decision needs to include reference to some contested technical claim, a committee comprising experts on the substantive issues and social scientists with expertise in the nature of science more generally, would be constituted to provide advice. Crucially, the committee would not be asked to settle the technical dispute by deciding who was right and who was wrong. Instead, the committee would be charged with producing, and making public, a summary of the degree of consensus or controversy about the topic in question and the content of that consensus. Policy-makers would then be expected to acknowledge and refer to this report in their decision-making but the decision on how to act would be for policy-makers alone. The members of the committee are called Owls because they will need to be able to view the claims in any controversy from both the natural and social scientific sides and thus, like owls, will need to be able to turn their heads through 180 degrees.

critics; these would also understand where the knowledge of experience-based experts is relevant but without falling into the trap of the notion of 'lay expertise' where esoteric matters are concerned. The social scientists would understand how non-establishment contributions to a technical debate should be handled without being too sympathetic or too elitist. Without this separation of powers, democracy would be unprotected from populism in one of the ways that it currently is protected—just! The danger of removing this check is illustrated by Trump and his colleagues discounting of climate change expertise based on an explicit discounting of technical expertise in general. Remember, the big danger is not the rejection of any specific claim coming out of the scientific and technological community, and certainly not the surreptitious and hypocritical rejection of any particular expert finding. The big danger is the explicit rejection of expertise *per se* as a moderator of governmental power and a source of checks and balances; such explicit rejection is an attempt to change the basic civic epistemology upon which collective decisions are based. The attempt to make such a change is accompanied by the 'proud proclamation' of the worthlessness of expertise, intended to de-legitimate expertise and change one of democracy's constitutive values.

To switch the example to the UK at the time of the Brexit debate, it was not Michael Gove's rejection of economic experts which was the problem—he might well have been right to reject the advice of economic experts (though events are suggesting he was wrong)—it was his actual or seeming dismissal of all experts that was the problem, a problem of a whole different order to the rejection of any specific piece of expert advice.[30] To go back again to Trump, his remedy for what he sees as flawed expert advice is not to seek better advice but to seek no advice at all—something quite different to the normal problems we have with expertise and one that entirely swamps the concern with making the advice of experts more or less efficacious by combining it with political and other values. Under the populist model there would be no expertise, efficacious or otherwise.

As intimated there is nothing in this model that is against the wider distribution of sources of scientific and technological advice and inviting more than the traditionally scientifically qualified elite to contribute. On

---

[30] In 2016, then Justice Secretary Michael Gove rejected gloomy predictions concerning the long-term economic and social effects of a possible vote in favour of Brexit by claiming that 'people in this country [UK] have had enough of experts'.

the contrary, over and over again the current authors have argued for the inclusion of experience-based experts in the body of expert advice-givers. A problem arises only if increasing the *diversity* of expertise is confused with the *democratisation* of expertise.[31] If no solution is found to the 'problem of extension'—that is, how to recognise the limits of expertise in any particular domain—then expertise disappears as anyone can be an expert and potential populists have free rein, at least in this regard.[32]

---

[31] Much of the controversy in the field of science and technology studies turns on this distinction. Both sides agree that some diversification of expertise is necessary; the difficulty arises when Collins and Evans (2002) suggested that technological decision-making in the public domain consists of two separate kinds of activity, which they labelled the technical and political phase. The technical phase concerns questions about the natural world and should, they argued, be open to all with relevant technical expertise—i.e. expertise would be diversified beyond that of formal science—but closed to those without such expertise. In contrast, the political phase, which might well refer to or make demands on the technical phase, should be open to all citizens. In response, critics argued the limitations put on participation in the technical phases were inconsistent with the democratisation of expertise (Wynne 2003; Jasanoff 2003), though the meaning of this phrase is often unclear. In particular, if all that is meant by this phrase is that expertise is to be held accountable to, and scrutinised by, citizens and/or their representatives then it is hard to see what the disagreement is about. On the other hand, if democratisation of expertise means that anyone can contribute to any expert debate then the position is intellectually untenable and inconsistent with claims made by its advocates when they write, for example, that:

> [T]he collective societal definition of what the issues and concerns are which should enjoy priority public attention and attempted resolution [are] not unconnected with specialist technical expertises, and where appropriate it should be informed by these, but it does not at all reduce to this. (Wynne 2007, 108)

Similar arguments and confusions reappear in the special issue of *Critical Policy Studies*, *referenced as* Collins et al. (2010).

[32] The problem of extension is first presented in Collins and Evans (2002), where it is contrasted with the problem of legitimacy. The problem of legitimacy arises when policy-makers place too much emphasis on narrow groups of scientific experts and the subsequent policy is rejected because it is not seen as adequately reflecting all the relevant points of view; legitimacy, so the argument goes, is only restored when the missing voices are included. This analysis, which is essentially a sociological critique of technocracy, was one of the most influential outputs of the social constructivist analysis of science. The problem of extension was first proposed as a hypothetical problem—is there a limit to the number or range of 'missing' voices and what happens if/when that limit is exceeded? The answer to this question was the distinction between technical and political phases, in which participation in the technical phase is limited to those with relevant specialist expertise but participation in the political phase remains open to all citizens.

CONCLUSION

To sum up, if we want to preserve the kinds of democratic societies we value, with the kind of checks and balances that we have, then we must teach our citizens a civic epistemology which allows a proper range of experts to give advice to government as an element in the constitution. That is, the right civic epistemology depends on citizens' understanding the relationship between the various elements of the fractal model of society roughly in the way they are currently understood in well-functioning pluralist democracies but with science and technology occupying a similar constitutional role to the legal system and the free press. Science should no longer find itself defending its position as a source of entertainment or a substitute for religion, as basic physics, astrophysics and cosmology are, nor as a driver of capitalism, but as a profession with a set of irreplaceable values and duties irrespective of outcomes. If expertise is dismissed out of hand, then that portion of the checks and balances disappears and we will no longer have the kind of society we have—imagine it! And if expertise is democratised—that is to say 'the people' are assumed to be as expert and informed about technical issues that have previously been seen as requiring many years of specialist training or experience to acquire—then the notion of expertise will disappear with the same dire consequences. None of this argues against a diversity of expertise where technical matters are concerned so long as the contributors are limited to those with specialist expertise, but this diversity has to be carefully assembled into something like a consensus or, at least, a consensual agreement to disagree with the planes of the disagreement and strength of disagreement set out, all driven by the norms of honesty and integrity not political or other values. Making non-scientific values the driver in an explicit way will destroy the very idea of science and remove one of the most important obstacles to the transformation of pluralist democracy into populism.

REFERENCES

Achen, Christopher R., and Larry M. Bartels. 2016. *Democracy for Realists: Why Elections Do Not Produce Responsive Government.* Princeton, NJ: Princeton University Press.

Bartels, Larry. 1996. Uninformed Votes: Information Effects in Presidential Elections. *American Political Science Review* 40: 194–230.

Brooks, David. 2017. The G.O.P. Is Rotting. *The New York Times*, December 7. https://www.nytimes.com/2017/12/07/opinion/the-gop-is-rotting.html

———. 2018. The End of the Two-Party System. *The New York Times*, February 12. https://www.nytimes.com/2018/02/12/opinion/trump-republicans-scarcity.html

Brown, Mark B. 2009. *Science in Democracy: Expertise, Institutions, and Representation.* Cambridge, MA: MIT Press.

Brubaker, Rogers. 2002. Ethnicity Without Groups. *European Journal of Sociology* 43 (2): 163–189.

Collins, Harry. 1990. *Artificial Experts: Social Knowledge and Intelligent Machines.* Inside Technology. Cambridge, MA: MIT Press.

———. 2004. Interactional Expertise as a Third Kind of Knowledge. *Phenomenology and the Cognitive Sciences* 3 (2): 125–143. https://doi.org/10.1023/B:PHEN.0000040824.89221.1a.

———. 2011. Language and Practice. *Social Studies of Science* 41 (2): 271–300. https://doi.org/10.1177/0306312711399665.

———. 2013. Three Dimensions of Expertise. *Phenomenology and the Cognitive Sciences* 12 (2): 253–273. https://doi.org/10.1007/s11097-011-9203-5.

———. 2015. Expertise Revisited, Part I—Interactional Expertise. *Studies in History and Philosophy of Science Part A* 54 (Dec.): 113–123.

———. 2016. An Imitation Game Concerning Gravitational Wave Physics. *ArXiv:1607.07373 [Physics]*, July. http://arxiv.org/abs/1607.07373

———. 2017. *Gravity's Kiss: The Discovery of Gravitational Waves.* Cambridge MA: MIT Press.

———. 2019. *Forms of Life: The Method and Meaning of Sociology.* Cambridge, MA: MIT Press.

Collins, Harry M., and Robert Evans. 2002. The Third Wave of Science Studies: Studies of Expertise and Experience. *Social Studies of Science* 32 (2): 235–296. https://doi.org/10.1177/0306312702032002003.

———. 2007. *Rethinking Expertise.* Chicago: University of Chicago Press.

———. 2014. Quantifying the Tacit: The Imitation Game and Social Fluency. *Sociology* 48 (1): 3–19. https://doi.org/10.1177/0038038512455735.

———. 2017a. *Why Democracies Need Science.* Cambridge and Malden, MA: Polity Press.

———. 2017b. Probes, Surveys, and the Ontology of the Social. *Journal of Mixed Methods Research* 11 (3): 328–341. https://doi.org/10.1177/1558689815619825.

Collins, Harry M., Robert Evans, Rodrigo Ribeiro, and Martin Hall. 2006. Experiments with Interactional Expertise. *Studies in History and Philosophy of Science Part A* 37 (4): 656–674. https://doi.org/10.1016/j.shpsa.2006.09.005.

Collins, Harry M., and Martin Kusch. 1998. *The Shape of Actions: What Humans and Machines Can Do.* Cambridge, MA: MIT Press.

Collins, Harry M., and Trevor J. Pinch. 1979. The Construction of the Paranormal: Nothing Unscientific Is Happening. *The Sociological Review* 27 (1_suppl): 237–270. https://doi.org/10.1111/j.1467-954X.1979.tb00064.x.

Collins, Harry M., Martin Weinel, and Robert Evans. 2010. The Politics and Policy of the Third Wave: New Technologies and Society. *Critical Policy Studies* 4 (2): 185–201. https://doi.org/10.1080/19460171.2010.490642.

Dreyfus, Hubert L. 1979. *What Computers Can't Do*. New York: MIT Press.

———. 1992. *What Computers Still Can't Do: A Critique of Artificial Reason*. Cambridge, MA: MIT Press.

Dreyfus, Hubert L., and Stuart E. Dreyfus. 1986. *Mind over Machine: The Power of Human Intuition and Expertise in the Era of the Computer*. New York: Free Press.

Dreyfus, Stuart E. 2004. The Five-Stage Model of Adult Skill Acquisition. *Bulletin of Science, Technology & Society* 24 (3): 177–181. https://doi.org/10.1177/0270467604264992.

Durant, Darrin. 2018. Servant or Partner? The Role of Expertise and Knowledge in Democracy. *The Conversation*, March 9. https://theconversation.com/servant-or-partner-the-role-of-expertise-and-knowledge-in-democracy-92026

———. 2019. Ignoring Experts. In *The Third Wave in Science and Technology Studies: Future Research Directions on the Study of Expertise and Experience*, ed. D. Caudill, S.N. Connolly, and M.E. Gorman. New York: Palgrave Macmillan. In Press.

Ericsson, K. Anders, Ralf T. Krampe, and Clemens Tesch-Römer. 1993. The Role of Deliberate Practice in the Acquisition of Expert Performance. *Psychological Review* 100 (3): 363–406. https://doi.org/10.1037/0033-295X.100.3.363.

Evans, Robert. 1999. *Macroeconomic Forecasting: A Sociological Appraisal*, Routledge Studies in the Modern World Economy. London and New York: Routledge.

———. 2014. Expert Advisers: Why Economic Forecasters Can Be Useful Even When They Are Wrong. In *Experts and Consensus in Social Science*, ed. Carlo Martini and Marcel Boumans, 233–252. New York: Springer.

Evans, Robert, Harry M. Collins, Martin Hall, Hannah O'Mahoney, and Martin Weinel. 2019. Bonfire Night and Burns Night: Using the Imitation Game to Research English and Scottish Identities. In *The Third Wave in the Sociology of Science: Selected Studies in Expertise and Experience*, ed. David Caudill, Michael E. Gorman, and Shannon N. Conley, 109–131. Palgrave Macmillan. https://doi.org/10.1007/978-3-030-14335-0.

Evans, Robert, and Helen Crocker. 2013. The Imitation Game as a Method for Exploring Knowledge(s) of Chronic Illness. *Methodological Innovations Online* 8 (1): 34–52. https://doi.org/10.4256/mio.2013.003.

Ezrahi, Yaron. 1990. *The Descent of Icarus: Science and the Transformation of Contemporary Democracy*. Cambridge, MA: Harvard University Press.

Frank, Thomas. 2008. *Wrecking Crew: How Conservatives Ruined the Government, Enriched Themselves, and Beggared the Nation*. New York: Holt Paperbacks.

Friedman, Jeffrey. 2006. Democratic Competence in Normative and Positive Theory: Neglected Implications of 'The Nature of Belief Systems in Mass Publics'. *Critical Review* 18: i–xliii.

Giles, Jim. 2006. Sociologist Fools Physics Judges. *Nature* 442 (7098): 8–8. https://doi.org/10.1038/442008a.

Gross, Paul R., Norman Levitt, and Martin W. Lewis, eds. 1997. *The Flight from Science and Reason*. Baltimore, MD and London: Johns Hopkins University Press.

Jasanoff, Sheila. 2003. Breaking the Waves in Science Studies: Comment on H.M. Collins and Robert Evans, 'The Third Wave of Science Studies'. *Social Studies of Science* 33 (3): 389–400. https://doi.org/10.1177/030631 27030333004.

———. 2005. *Designs on Nature: Science and Democracy in Europe and the United States*. Princeton, NJ and Oxford: Princeton University Press.

Lave, Jean, and Etienne Wenger. 1991. *Situated Learning: Legitimate Peripheral Participation*, Learning in Doing. Cambridge and New York: Cambridge University Press.

Levitsky, Steven, and Daniel Ziblatt. 2018. *How Democracies Die*. 1st ed. New York: Crown.

Miller, Clark A. 2008. Civic Epistemologies: Constituting Knowledge and Order in Political Communities. *Sociology Compass* 2 (6): 1896–1919. https://doi. org/10.1111/j.1751-9020.2008.00175.x.

Mounk, Yascha. 2018a. How Populist Uprisings Could Bring down Liberal Democracy | Mounk, Yascha. *The Guardian*, March 4, sec. Opinion. https://www.theguardian.com/commentisfree/2018/mar/04/shock-system-liberaldemocracy-populism.

———. 2018b. *The People VS. Democracy: Why Our Freedom Is in Danger and How to Save It*. Cambridge, MA: Harvard University Press.

Pielke, Roger A. 2007. *The Honest Broker: Making Sense of Science in Policy and Politics*. Cambridge and New York: Cambridge University Press.

Polanyi, Michael. 1966. *The Tacit Dimension*. Chicago and London: University of Chicago Press.

Runciman, David. 2018. *How Democracy Ends*. London: Profile Books.

Sarewitz, Daniel. 2016. Saving Science. *The New Atlantis* 49: 4–40.

Somin, Ilya. 2013. *Democracy and Political Ignorance*. Stanford, CA: Stanford University Press.

Thorpe, Charles. 2008. Political Theory in Science and Technology Studies. In *The Handbook of Science and Technology Studies*, ed. Edward J. Hackett, Olga Amsterdamska, Michael Lynch, and Judy Wajcman, 63–82. Cambridge MA: MIT Press.

Wehrens, Rik. 2014. The Potential of the Imitation Game Method in Exploring Healthcare Professionals' Understanding of the Lived Experiences and Practical

Challenges of Chronically Ill Patients. *Health Care Analysis* 23 (3): 253–271. https://doi.org/10.1007/s10728-014-0273-8.

Wehrens, Rik, and Bethany Hipple Walters. 2017. Understanding Each Other in the Medical Encounter: Exploring Therapists' and Patients' Understanding of Each Other's Experiential Knowledge through the Imitation Game. *Health*, August. https://doi.org/10.1177/1363459317721100.

Wynne, Brian. 2003. Seasick on the Third Wave? Subverting the Hegemony of Propositionalism: Response to Collins & Evans (2002). *Social Studies of Science* 33 (3): 401–417. https://doi.org/10.1177/03063127030333005.

———. 2007. Public Participation in Science and Technology: Performing and Obscuring a Political–Conceptual Category Mistake. *East Asian Science, Technology and Society: An International Journal* 1 (1): 99–110. https://doi.org/10.1007/s12280-007-9004-7.

REFERENCES

Achen, Christopher R., and Larry M. Bartels. 2016. *Democracy for Realists: Why Elections Do Not Produce Responsive Government*. Princeton, NJ: Princeton University Press.

Arditi, B. 2003. Populism, or Politics at the Edges of Democracy. *Contemporary Politics* 9 (1): 17–31.

Bartels, Larry. 1996. Uninformed Votes: Information Effects in Presidential Elections. *American Political Science Review* 40: 194–230.

Bijker, Wiebe E. 2007. Dikes and Dams, Thick with Politics. *Isis* 98 (1): 109–123. https://doi.org/10.1086/512835.

Bloor, David. 1973. Wittgenstein and Mannheim on the Sociology of Mathematics. *Studies in History and Philosophy of Science Part A* 4 (2): 173–191. https://doi.org/10.1016/0039-3681(73)90003-4.

———. 1991. *Knowledge and Social Imagery*. 2nd ed. Chicago: University of Chicago Press.

Brooks, David. 2017. The G.O.P. Is Rotting. *The New York Times*, December 7. https://www.nytimes.com/2017/12/07/opinion/the-gop-is-rotting.html

———. 2018. The End of the Two-Party System. *The New York Times*, February 12. https://www.nytimes.com/2018/02/12/opinion/trump-republicans-scarcity.html

Brown, Mark B. 2009. *Science in Democracy: Expertise, Institutions, and Representation*. Cambridge, MA: MIT Press.

Brubaker, Rogers. 2002. Ethnicity Without Groups. *European Journal of Sociology* 43 (2): 163–189.

Callon, Michel. 1986. Some Elements of a Sociology of Translation: Domestication of the Scallops and the Fishermen of St Brieuc Bay. In *Power, Action and Belief:*

© The Author(s) 2020
H. Collins et al., *Experts and the Will of the People*,
https://doi.org/10.1007/978-3-030-26983-8

A New Sociology of Knowledge? ed. John Law, 196–223. London: Routledge. http://ionesco.sciences-po.fr/com/moodledata/3/Callon_Sociology Translation.pdf.

Collins, Harry. 1974. The TEA Set: Tacit Knowledge and Scientific Networks. *Science Studies* 4 (2): 165–185.

———. 1975. The Seven Sexes: A Study in the Sociology of a Phenomenon, or the Replication of Experiments in Physics. *Sociology* 9 (2): 205–224. https://doi.org/10.1177/003803857500900202.

———. 1990. *Artificial Experts: Social Knowledge and Intelligent Machines.* Inside Technology. Cambridge, MA: MIT Press.

———. 1985/1992. *Changing Order: Replication and Induction in Scientific Practice.* Chicago: University of Chicago Press. [1992 = second edition]

———. 2004. Interactional Expertise as a Third Kind of Knowledge. *Phenomenology and the Cognitive Sciences* 3 (2): 125–143. https://doi.org/10.1023/B:PHEN.0000040824.89221.1a.

———. 2010. *Tacit and Explicit Knowledge.* Chicago and London: University of Chicago Press.

———. 2011. Language and Practice. *Social Studies of Science* 41 (2): 271–300. https://doi.org/10.1177/0306312711399665.

———. 2013. Three Dimensions of Expertise. *Phenomenology and the Cognitive Sciences* 12 (2): 253–273. https://doi.org/10.1007/s11097-011-9203-5.

———. 2015. Expertise Revisited, Part I—Interactional Expertise. *Studies in History and Philosophy of Science Part A* 54 (Dec.): 113–123.

———. 2016. An Imitation Game Concerning Gravitational Wave Physics. *ArXiv:1607.07373 [Physics]*, July. http://arxiv.org/abs/1607.07373

———. 2017. *Gravity's Kiss: The Discovery of Gravitational Waves.* Cambridge MA: MIT Press.

———. 2018. *Artifictional Intelligence: Against the Humanity's Surrender to Computers.* Cambridge: Polity Press.

———. 2019. *Forms of Life: The Method and Meaning of Sociology.* Cambridge, MA: MIT Press.

Collins, Harry M., Andrew Bartlett, and Luis Reyes-Galindo. 2017a. Demarcating Fringe Science for Policy. *Perspectives on Science* 25 (4): 411–438. https://doi.org/10.1162/POSC_a_00248.

Collins, Harry M., and Robert Evans. 2002. The Third Wave of Science Studies: Studies of Expertise and Experience. *Social Studies of Science* 32 (2): 235–296. https://doi.org/10.1177/0306312702032002003.

———. 2003. King Canute Meets the Beach Boys: Responses to the Third Wave. *Social Studies of Science* 33 (3): 435–452. https://doi.org/10.1177/03063127030333007.

———. 2007. *Rethinking Expertise.* Chicago: University of Chicago Press.

———. 2014. Quantifying the Tacit: The Imitation Game and Social Fluency. *Sociology* 48 (1): 3–19. https://doi.org/10.1177/0038038512455735.

———. 2017a. *Why Democracies Need Science*. Cambridge and Malden, MA: Polity Press.

———. 2017b. Probes, Surveys, and the Ontology of the Social. *Journal of Mixed Methods Research* 11 (3): 328–341. https://doi.org/10.1177/1558689815619825.

Collins, Harry M., Robert Evans, Rodrigo Ribeiro, and Martin Hall. 2006. Experiments with Interactional Expertise. *Studies in History and Philosophy of Science Part A* 37 (4): 656–674. https://doi.org/10.1016/j.shpsa.2006.09.005.

Collins, Harry, Robert Evans, and Martin Weinel. 2017b. STS as Science or Politics? *Social Studies of Science* 47 (4): 580–586. https://doi.org/10.1177/0306312717710131.

Collins, Harry M., Robert Evans, Martin Weinel, Jennifer Lyttleton-Smith, Andrew Bartlett, and Martin Hall. 2017c. The Imitation Game and the Nature of Mixed Methods. *Journal of Mixed Methods Research* 11 (4): 510–527. https://doi.org/10.1177/1558689815619824.

Collins, Harry M., Sam Finn, and Patrick Sutton. 2001. What Is TWAP? Three Notes on the American Election in the Year 2000. *Social Studies of Science* 31 (3): 428–436.

Collins, Harry M., and Martin Kusch. 1998. *The Shape of Actions: What Humans and Machines Can Do*. Cambridge, MA: MIT Press.

Collins, Harry M., and Trevor J. Pinch. 1979. The Construction of the Paranormal: Nothing Unscientific Is Happening. *The Sociological Review* 27 (1_suppl): 237–270. https://doi.org/10.1111/j.1467-954X.1979.tb00064.x.

———. 2005. *Dr. Golem How to Think about Medicine*. Chicago: University of Chicago Press.

Collins, Harry M, and Trevor Pinch. 2010. *The Golem at Large: What You Should Know about Technology*. 6th Print. Cambridge: Cambridge University Press.

Collins, Harry M., Martin Weinel, and Robert Evans. 2010. The Politics and Policy of the Third Wave: New Technologies and Society. *Critical Policy Studies* 4 (2): 185–201. https://doi.org/10.1080/19460171.2010.490642.

Dahl, Robert. 1956. *A Preface to Democratic Theory*. Chicago: University of Chicago Press.

Dewey, John. 1954 [1927]. *The Public and its Problems*. Athens, OH: Swallow Press. (Original work published 1927.)

Diamond, Larry, and Marc F. Plattner, eds. 2010. *Democratization in Africa: Progress and Retreat*. Baltimore, MD: Johns Hopkins University Press.

Douglas, Heather E. 2009. *Science, Policy, and the Value-Free Ideal*. Pittsburgh, PA: University of Pittsburgh Press.

Douthat, Ross. 2018. The Pull of Populism. *The New York Times*, February 14. https://www.nytimes.com/2018/02/14/opinion/trump-populism-republican-party.html

Dreyfus, Hubert L. 1979. *What Computers Can't Do*. New York: MIT Press.
———. 1992. *What Computers Still Can't Do: A Critique of Artificial Reason*. Cambridge, MA: MIT Press.
Dreyfus, Hubert L., and Stuart E. Dreyfus. 1986. *Mind over Machine: The Power of Human Intuition and Expertise in the Era of the Computer*. New York: Free Press.
Dreyfus, Stuart E. 2004. The Five-Stage Model of Adult Skill Acquisition. *Bulletin of Science, Technology & Society* 24 (3): 177–181. https://doi.org/10.1177/0270467604264992.
Durant, Darrin. 2011. Models of Democracy in Social Studies of Science. *Social Studies of Science* 41 (5): 691–714.
———. 2016. The Undead Linear Model of Expertise. In *Political Legitimacy, Science and Social Authority: Knowledge and Action in Liberal Democracies*, ed. M. Heazle and J. Kane, 17–37. London: Routledge.
———. 2017. Who Are You Calling 'Anti-science'? How Science Serves Social and Political Agendas. *The Conversation*, July 31. https://theconversation.com/who-are-you-calling-anti-science-how-science-serves-social-and-political-agendas-74755. [Reprinted in *The Conversation Yearbook 2017: 50 Standout Articles from Australia's Top Thinkers*. Edited by John Watson. The Conversation Trust; 66–71]
———. 2018. Servant or Partner? The Role of Expertise and Knowledge in Democracy. *The Conversation*, March 9. https://theconversation.com/servant-or-partner-the-role-of-expertise-and-knowledge-in-democracy-92026
———. 2019. Ignoring Experts. In *The Third Wave in Science and Technology Studies: Future Research Directions on the Study of Expertise and Experience*, ed. D. Caudill, S.N. Connolly, and M.E. Gorman. New York: Palgrave Macmillan. In Press.
Durkheim, Émile. 1915. *The Elementary Forms of Religious Life*. Edited by Mark Sydney Cladis and translated by Carol Cosman. Oxford World's Classics. Oxford: Oxford University Press.
———. 2013. *The Division of Labour in Society*. Edited by Steven Lukes and translated by W.D. Halls. Basingstoke: Palgrave Macmillan.
Epstein, Steven. 1996. *Impure Science: AIDS, Activism, and the Politics of Knowledge*. Berkeley: University of California Press.
Ericsson, K. Anders, Ralf T. Krampe, and Clemens Tesch-Römer. 1993. The Role of Deliberate Practice in the Acquisition of Expert Performance. *Psychological Review* 100 (3): 363–406. https://doi.org/10.1037/0033-295X.100.3.363.
Evans, Robert. 1999. *Macroeconomic Forecasting: A Sociological Appraisal*, Routledge Studies in the Modern World Economy. London and New York: Routledge.
———. 2014. Expert Advisers: Why Economic Forecasters Can Be Useful Even When They Are Wrong. In *Experts and Consensus in Social Science*, ed. Carlo Martini and Marcel Boumans, 233–252. New York: Springer.

Evans, Robert, Harry M. Collins, Martin Hall, Hannah O'Mahoney, and Martin Weinel. 2019. Bonfire Night and Burns Night: Using the Imitation Game to Research English and Scottish Identities. In *The Third Wave in the Sociology of Science: Selected Studies in Expertise and Experience*, ed. David Caudill, Michael E. Gorman, and Shannon N. Conley, 109–131. Palgrave Macmillan. https://doi.org/10.1007/978-3-030-14335-0.

Evans, Robert, Harry Collins, Martin Weinel, Jennifer Lyttleton-Smith, Hannah O'Mahoney, and Willow Leonard-Clarke. 2018. Groups and Individuals: Conformity and Diversity in the Performance of Gendered Identities. *The British Journal of Sociology*. https://doi.org/10.1111/1468-4446.12507.

Evans, Robert, and Helen Crocker. 2013. The Imitation Game as a Method for Exploring Knowledge(s) of Chronic Illness. *Methodological Innovations Online* 8 (1): 34–52. https://doi.org/10.4256/mio.2013.003.

Eyal, Gil, Ivan Szelenyi, and Eleanor R. Townsley. 2001. *Making Capitalism Without Capitalists: The New Ruling Elites in Eastern Europe*. London: Verso.

Ezrahi, Yaron. 1990. *The Descent of Icarus: Science and the Transformation of Contemporary Democracy*. Cambridge, MA: Harvard University Press.

Felt, Ulrike, Rayvon Fouche, Clark Miller, and Laurel Smith-Doerr, eds. 2017. *The Handbook of Science and Technology Studies*. 4th ed. Cambridge, MA: MIT Press.

Fleck, Ludwik. 2008. *Genesis and Development of a Scientific Fact*. Translated by Thaddeus J. Trenn and Fred Bradley. Repr. 11. Aufl (First published in German in 1935). Sociology of Science. Chicago: University of Chicago Press.

Frank, Thomas. 2008. *Wrecking Crew: How Conservatives Ruined the Government, Enriched Themselves, and Beggared the Nation*. New York: Holt Paperbacks.

Franklin, Allan, and Harry Collins. 2016. Two Kinds of Case Study and a New Agreement. In *The Philosophy of Historical Case Studies, Boston Studies in the Philosophy of Science*, ed. T. Sauer and R. Scholl, 95–121. Dordrecht: Springer.

Freedland, Jonathan. 2017. The Year of Trump Has Laid Bare the US Constitution's Serious Flaws. *The Guardian*, December 30, UK edition, sec. Opinion.

———. 2018. Brexit Reveals Our Political System Is Failing. The 48% Must Have a Voice. *The Guardian*, February 9, UK edition, sec. Opinion. https://www.theguardian.com/commentisfree/2018/feb/09/brexit-political-system-failing-48-per-cent-theresa-may-corbyn-betrayed

Friedman, Jeffrey. 2006. Democratic Competence in Normative and Positive Theory: Neglected Implications of 'The Nature of Belief Systems in Mass Publics'. *Critical Review* 18: i–xliii.

Fuller, Steve. 2016. Embrace the Inner Fox: Post-Truth as the STS Symmetry Principle Universalized. *Social Epistemology Review and Reply Collective*, December 25. https://social-epistemology.com/2016/12/25/embrace-the-inner-fox-post-truth-as-the-sts-symmetry-principle-universalized-steve-fuller/

Funtowicz, Silvio O., and Jerome R. Ravetz. 1993. Science for the Post-Normal Age. *Futures* 25 (7): 739–755. https://doi.org/10.1016/0016-3287(93)90022-L.

Garfinkel, Harold. 2011. *Studies in Ethnomethodology*. Reprinted. Cambridge: Polity Press.

Geffen, Nathan. 2010. *Debunking Delusions: The Inside Story of the Treatment Action Campaign*. Johannesburg: Jacana Media.

Giles, Jim. 2006. Sociologist Fools Physics Judges. *Nature* 442 (7098): 8–8. https://doi.org/10.1038/442008a.

Gouldner, Alvin, W. 1954. *Patterns of Industrial Bureaucracy*. New York: Free Press.

Gross, Paul R., and N. Levitt. 1998. *Higher Superstition: The Academic Left and Its Quarrels with Science*. Johns Hopkins Paperbacks ed. Baltimore, MD: Johns Hopkins University Press.

Gross, Paul R., Norman Levitt, and Martin W. Lewis, eds. 1997. *The Flight from Science and Reason*. Baltimore, MD and London: Johns Hopkins University Press.

Habermas, Jürgen. 1996. *Between Facts and Norms: Contributions to a Discourse Theory of Law and Democracy*. Translated by William Rehg. Cambridge, MA: MIT Press.

Hackett, E.J., O. Amsterdamska, M. Lynch, and J. Wajcman, eds. 2007. *Handbook of Science and Technology Studies*. 3rd ed. Cambridge, MA: MIT Press.

Held, David. 1995. *Democracy and the Global Order: From the Modern State to Cosmopolitan Governance*. Stanford, CA: Stanford University Press.

———. 2006. *Models of Democracy*. 3rd ed. Cambridge: Polity Press.

Hilgartner, Stephen. 2000. *Science on Stage: Expert Advice as Public Drama, Writing Science*. Stanford, CA: Stanford University Press.

Holton, G. 1978. *The Scientific Imagination*. Cambridge: Cambridge University Press.

Irwin, Alan. 1995. *Citizen Science: A Study of People, Expertise, and Sustainable Development*, Environment and Society. London and New York: Routledge.

Jacobson, Howard. 2017. The Next Time Jacob Rees-Mogg Is Given Screen Time, I Will Break the Television. *The Guardian*, October 21. https://www.theguardian.com/books/2017/oct/21/jacob-rees-mogg-given-screen-time

Jasanoff, Sheila. 1990. *The Fifth Branch: Science Advisers as Policy-Makers*. Cambridge, MA: Harvard University Press.

———. 2003. Breaking the Waves in Science Studies: Comment on H.M. Collins and Robert Evans, 'The Third Wave of Science Studies'. *Social Studies of Science* 33 (3): 389–400. https://doi.org/10.1177/03063127030333004.

———. 2005. *Designs on Nature: Science and Democracy in Europe and the United States*. Princeton, NJ and Oxford: Princeton University Press.

Jasanoff, Sheila, and Hilton R. Simmet. 2017. No Funeral Bells: Public Reason in a "Post-Truth" Age. *Social Studies of Science* 47 (5): 751–770. https://doi.org/10.1177/0306312717731936.

Judis, John B. 2016. *The Populist Explosion: How the Great Recession Transformed American and European Politics*. New York: Columbia Global Reports.

Keane, John. 2018. Post-Truth Politics and Why the Antidote Isn't Simply 'Fact-checking' and Truth. *The Conversation*, March 23. https://theconversation.com/post-truth-politics-and-why-the-antidote-isnt-simply-fact-checking-and-truth-87364

Knorr-Cetina, Karin. 1981. *The Manufacture of Knowledge*. Oxford: Pergamon Press.

Koertge, Noretta, ed. 2000. *A House Built on Sand: Exposing Postmodernist Myths about Science*. New York: Oxford University Press.

Kuhn, Thomas S. 1962. *The Structure of Scientific Revolutions*. Chicago: University of Chicago Press.

Labinger, Jay A., and Harry M. Collins. 2001. *The One Culture?* Chicago: University of Chicago Press. http://www.press.uchicago.edu/ucp/books/book/chicago/O/bo3634845.html.

Laclau, Ernesto. 2005. *On Populist Reason*. London: Verso.

Latour, Bruno. 1993. *We Have Never Been Modern*. Cambridge, MA: Harvard University Press.

———. 2003. *Science in Action: How to Follow Scientists and Engineers through Society*. 11th Print. Cambridge, MA: Harvard University Press.

Latour, Bruno, and Steve Woolgar. 1979. *Laboratory Life: The Social Construction of Scientific Facts*, Sage Library of Social Research, vol. 80. Beverly Hills: Sage Publications.

Lave, Jean, and Etienne Wenger. 1991. *Situated Learning: Legitimate Peripheral Participation*, Learning in Doing. Cambridge and New York: Cambridge University Press.

Leonard, David, and Stuart A. Thompson. 2017. Trump's Lies. *The New York Times*, December 14. https://www.nytimes.com/interactive/2017/06/23/opinion/trumps-lies.html?action=click&contentCollection=Politics&module=RelatedCoverage&region=EndOfArticle&pgtype=article

Levitsky, Steven, and Daniel Ziblatt. 2018. *How Democracies Die*. 1st ed. New York: Crown.

Lijphart, Arend. 1999. *Patterns of Democracy: Government Forms and Performance in Thirty-Six Countries*. New Haven, CT: Yale University Press.

———. 2012. *Patterns of Democracy: Government Forms and Performance in Thirty-Six Countries*. 2nd updated and expanded ed. New Haven, CT: Yale University Press.

Lippmann, Walter. 1993. *The Phantom Public*. New Brunswick, NJ: Transaction Publishers.

———. 2007. *Public Opinion*. La Vergne, TN: BN Publishing.

MacKenzie, Donald A. 1981. *Statistics in Britain, 1865–1930*. Edinburgh: Edinburgh University Press.

Marres, Noortje. 2007. The Issues Deserve More Credit: A Pragmatist Contribution to the Study of Public Involvement in Controversy. *Social Studies of Science* 37 (5): 759–780.

Martin, Emily. 1991. The Egg and the Sperm: How Science Has Constructed a Romance Based on Stereotypical Male-Female Roles. *Signs* 16 (3): 485–501.

Medawar, Peter. 1967. *The Art of the Soluble.* London: Methuen.

Merton, Robert King. 1973. *The Sociology of Science: Theoretical and Empirical Investigations.* Chicago: University of Chicago Press.

Miller, Clark A. 2008. Civic Epistemologies: Constituting Knowledge and Order in Political Communities. *Sociology Compass* 2 (6): 1896–1919. https://doi.org/10.1111/j.1751-9020.2008.00175.x.

Mol, Annemarie. 2003. *The Body Multiple: Ontology in Medical Practice.* Durham, NC: Duke University Press.

Mouffe, Chantal. 2000. *The Democratic Paradox.* London: Verso.

———. 2018. *For a Left Populism.* London: Verso.

Mounk, Yascha. 2018a. How Populist Uprisings Could Bring down Liberal Democracy | Mounk, Yascha. *The Guardian*, March 4, sec. Opinion. https://www.theguardian.com/commentisfree/2018/mar/04/shock-system-liberal-democracy-populism

———. 2018b. *The People VS. Democracy: Why Our Freedom Is in Danger and How to Save It.* Cambridge, MA: Harvard University Press.

Mudde, Cas. 2017. The Problem with Populism. *The Guardian*, February 27. https://www.theguardian.com/commentisfree/2015/feb/17/problem-populism-syriza-podemos-dark-side-europe

———. 2018. How Can Liberals Defeat Populism. *The Guardian*, February 13. https://www.theguardian.com/commentisfree/2018/feb/13/liberals-populism-world-forum-democracy-5-ideas

Mudde, Cas, and Cristobal Rovira Kaltwasser. 2017. *Populism: A Very Short Introduction.* New York: Oxford University Press.

Müller, Jan-Werner. 2017. *What Is Populism?* London: Penguin Books.

Newman, N., Fletcher, R., Kalogeropoulos, A., Levy, D., and Kleis Nielsen, R. 2017. Reuters Digital News Report 2017. Oxford: Reuters Institute for the Study of Journalism. Retrieved from http://www.digitalnewsreport.org/.

Oreskes, Naomi, and Erik M. Conway. 2010. *Merchants of Doubt: How a Handful of Scientists Obscured the Truth on Issues from Tobacco Smoke to Global Warming.* 1st U.S. ed. New York: Bloomsbury Press.

Osborne, Roger. 2012. *Of the People, by the People: A New History of Democracy.* London: Pimlico.

Ottinger, Gwen. 2013. *Refining Expertise: How Responsible Engineers Subvert Environmental Justice Challenges.* New York: New York University Press.

Oudshoorn, Nelly. 1994. *Beyond the Natural Body: An Archeology of Sex Hormones.* London: Routledge.

Pettit, Philip. 1997. *Republicanism: A Theory of Freedom and Government*. Oxford: Oxford University Press.

Pielke, Roger A. 2007. *The Honest Broker: Making Sense of Science in Policy and Politics*. Cambridge and New York: Cambridge University Press.

Pitkin, Hanna Fenichel. 1967. *The Concept of Representation*. Berkeley: University of California Press.

———. 1998. Are Freedom and Liberty Twins? *Political Theory* 16: 523–552.

———. 2004. Representation and Democracy: A Uneasy Alliance. In *Politics, Judgment, Action*, ed. Dean Mathiowetz, 225–232. Milton Park: Routledge.

Polanyi, Michael. 1966. *The Tacit Dimension*. Chicago and London: University of Chicago Press.

Popper, Karl R. 2002. *The Logic of Scientific Discovery*. London and New York: Routledge.

Rawls, John. 1993. *Political Liberalism*. Expanded ed. Columbia Classics in Philosophy. New York: Columbia University Press.

Rip, Arie. 2003. Constructing Expertise: In a Third Wave of Science Studies? *Social Studies of Science* 33 (3): 419–434. https://doi.org/10.1177/03063127030333006.

Roth, Kenneth. 2017. The Dangerous Rise of Populism: Global Attacks on Human Rights Values. In *World Report 2017*, ed. Human Rights Watch. https://www.hrw.org/sites/default/files/world_report_download/wr2017-web.pdf

Rousseau, Jean-Jacques. 1987 [1762]. On the Social Contract, or Principles of Political Rights. In *Basic Political Writings*, trans. and ed. Donald A. Cres, 139–227. Indianapolis, IN: Hackett.

Rudwick, M. 1985. *The Great Devonian Controversy: The Shaping of Scientific Knowledge Among Gentlemanly Specialists*. Chicago: University of Chicago Press.

Runciman, David. 2018. *How Democracy Ends*. London: Profile Books.

Salter, Liora. 1988. *Mandated Science: Science and Scientists in the Making of Standards*. Dordrecht: Kluwer.

Sarewitz, Daniel. 2016. Saving Science. *The New Atlantis* 49: 4–40.

Sartori, Giovanni. 1965. *Democratic Theory*. New York: Praeger.

Shapin, Steven. 1979. The Politics of Observation: Cerebral Anatomy and Social Interests in the Edinburgh Phrenology Disputes. *The Sociological Review* 27 (May): 139–178. https://doi.org/10.1111/j.1467-954X.1979.tb00061.x.

———. 2007. *A Social History of Truth: Civility and Science in Seventeenth-Century England*. 4th Print. Science and Its Conceptual Foundations. Chicago: University of Chicago Press.

Shapin, Steven, and Simon Schaffer. 1985/2011. *Leviathan and the Air-Pump: Hobbes, Boyle, and the Experimental Life*. [First published 1985]. Princeton, NJ: Princeton University Press.

Sismondo, Sergio. 2017a. Post-Truth? *Social Studies of Science* 47 (1): 3–6. https://doi.org/10.1177/0306312717692076.

———. 2017b. Casting a Wider Net: A Reply to Collins, Evans and Weinel. *Social Studies of Science* 47 (4): 587–592. https://doi.org/10.1177/0306312717721410.

Sokal, Alan D., and Jean Bricmont. 1999. *Fashionable Nonsense: Postmodern Intellectuals' Abuse of Science.* 1st paperback ed. New York: St. Martin's Press.

Somin, Ilya. 2013. *Democracy and Political Ignorance.* Stanford, CA: Stanford University Press.

Sparrow, Jeff. 2018. *Trigger Warnings: Political Correctness and the Rise of the Right.* Brunswick, VIC: SCRIBE.

Szelenyi, Ivan. 2016. Weber's Theory of Domination and Post-communist Capitalisms. *Theory and Society* 45: 1–24.

Taylor, Charles. 1998. The Dynamic of Democratic Exclusion. *Journal of Democracy* 9 (4): 143–156.

Temelkuran, Ece. 2019. *How to Lose a Country: The 7 Steps from Democracy to Dictatorship.* London: 4th Estate.

Thorpe, Charles. 2008. Political Theory in Science and Technology Studies. In *The Handbook of Science and Technology Studies,* ed. Edward J. Hackett, Olga Amsterdamska, Michael Lynch, and Judy Wajcman, 63–82. Cambridge MA: MIT Press.

Turner, Stephen P. 2003. *Liberal Democracy 3.0: Civil Society in an Age of Experts,* Theory, Culture & Society. London and Thousand Oaks, CA: SAGE Publications.

Urbinati, Nadia. 2006a. *Representative Democracy: Principles and Genealogy.* Chicago: University of Chicago Press.

———. 2006b. Political Representation as a Democratic Process. Edited by K Palonen. *Redescriptions—Yearbook of Political Thought and Conceptual History* 10 (1): 18–40.

Waldron, J. 2012. Democracy. In *The Oxford Handbook of Political Philosophy,* ed. David Estlund, 197–203. Oxford: Oxford University Press.

Warren, Mark. 1996. What Should We Expect from More Democracy?: Radically Democratic Responses to Politics. *Political Theory* 24 (2): 241–270.

Warren, Mark, and Hilary Pearse, eds. 2008. *Designing Deliberative Democracy: The British Columbia Citizens' Assembly.* Cambridge and New York: Cambridge University Press.

Weale, Albert. 2018. *The Will of the People: A Modern Myth.* Cambridge: Polity Press.

Wehrens, Rik. 2014. The Potential of the Imitation Game Method in Exploring Healthcare Professionals' Understanding of the Lived Experiences and Practical Challenges of Chronically Ill Patients. *Health Care Analysis* 23 (3): 253–271. https://doi.org/10.1007/s10728-014-0273-8.

Wehrens, Rik, and Bethany Hipple Walters. 2017. Understanding Each Other in the Medical Encounter: Exploring Therapists' and Patients' Understanding of Each Other's Experiential Knowledge through the Imitation Game. *Health*, August. https://doi.org/10.1177/1363459317721100.

Winch, Peter. 1958. *The Idea of a Social Science and Its Relation to Philosophy*, Studies in Philosophical Psychology. London and New York: Routledge & Kegan Paul.

———. 1964. Understanding a Primitive Society. *American Philosophical Quarterly* 1 (4): 307–324. https://doi.org/10.2307/20009143.

Winograd, Terry, and Fernando Flores. 1987. *Understanding Computers and Cognition: A New Foundation for Design*. Reading, MA: Addison-Wesley.

Wittgenstein, Ludwig. 1953. *Philosophical Investigations*. Translated by G.E.M Anscombe. Oxford: Blackwell.

World Forum for Democracy. 2017. *Is Populism a Problem?* https://rm.coe.int/world-forum-for-democracy-2017-final-report/16807840c7

Wynne, Brian. 1992. Misunderstood Misunderstanding: Social Identities and Public Uptake of Science. *Public Understanding of Science* 1 (3): 281–304. https://doi.org/10.1088/0963-6625/1/3/004.

———. 2003. Seasick on the Third Wave? Subverting the Hegemony of Propositionalism: Response to Collins & Evans (2002). *Social Studies of Science* 33 (3): 401–417. https://doi.org/10.1177/03063127030333005.

———. 2007. Public Participation in Science and Technology: Performing and Obscuring a Political–Conceptual Category Mistake. *East Asian Science, Technology and Society: An International Journal* 1 (1): 99–110. https://doi.org/10.1007/s12280-007-9004-7.

Printed by Printforce, the Netherlands